D0383897

GUIDE TO
MAKING MONEY
How To Do It Yourself

By The Editors of

Canadian MoneySaver

ALL NEW EDITION
INCLUDES
1987 TAX REFORM

Copyright © 1985, 1987 by Canadian Money Saver Inc.
P.O. Box 370
Bath, Ontario
Canada K0H 1G0

All rights reserved.

Printed in Canada.

Reproduction or translation of any part of this work beyond that permitted by the Copyright Act without the permission of the copyright owner is unlawful. Requests for permission or further information should be addressed to the Permissions Department, Canadian Money Saver Inc.

Brief passages may be quoted without permission provided credit is given in the following form: "Guide to Making Money" by the Editors of "Canadian MoneySaver", Box 370, Bath, Ontario K0H 1G0.

This publication is designed to provide accurate and authoritative information in regard to the subject matter covered. It is sold with the understanding that the authors and the publisher cannot be held responsible for errors or omissions.

First Edition: October, 1985
          Reprinted: March 1986, November 1986, June 1987
Second Edition: September, 1987
Cover: Joanne Guindon-Bedard, Nicole's Photography, Kingston, Ontario
Typeset: Our Money Inc., Bath, Ontario

$9.95

Canadian Cataloguing in Publication Data
Main entry under title:

Guide to making money

2nd ed.
ISBN 0-920937-02-0

1. Finance, Personal.   2. Investments.   I. Canadian MoneySaver.

HG179.G856 1987   332.024'01   C87-094790-7

Contents

About The Authors 7

Preface 9

CHAPTER 1: Personal Money Management 11
INTRODUCTION
YOUR FINANCIAL PLAN
  • Phase One: Net Worth
  • Phase Two: Goal Setting
  • Phase Three: Cash Flow Forecasting
  • Phase Four: Budgeting
FINANCIAL CONCEPTS
  • Inflation
  • Interest
  • Marginal Tax Rate
  • Real Return
  • Retirement Income
INVESTMENT CONCEPTS
  • Considerations of Investment Decisions
  • Risk and Reward
THE PRIORITY APPROACH
  • Stage One
  • Stage Two
  • Stages Three and Four
INVESTMENT USES
SUMMARY

CHAPTER 2: Taxation and Investments 43
INTRODUCTION
FIGURING OUT YOUR INCOME TAX BRACKET
INVESTMENT INCOME DEDUCTION
  • Monitor Corporation Investments
  • Spousal Transfers
  • For Seniors
  • Borrow For Foreign Investments
INTEREST INCOME AND THE THREE-YEAR ACCRUAL RATE
THE DIVIDEND VERSUS INTEREST DEBATE
MORE ABOUT CAPITAL GAINS
USING THE CAPITAL GAINS EXEMPTION FOR FUN AND PROFIT
  • Personal Acquisitions Of Assets
  • Sale Of Marketable Securities To An RRSP
  • Shareholders' Agreements And Wills
THE TRANSFER OF DIVIDENDS ELECTION
TAX SHELTERS
A FINAL WORD ABOUT INVESTMENTS

CHAPTER 3: The Strategy For Investing 57

PART I. GETTING RICH SLOWLY
BASIC PRINCIPLES
- Four Ingredients Of Wealth
- A Strategy For Getting Rich Slowly...Fast
- How The World Works: A Crash Course In Economics
- Along The Way To Financial Freedom

PART II. FIRST LEG OF THE STRATEGY
EAST POOL/WEST POOL
- How To Build The East Pool
- How To Build The West Pool
- East Pool/West Pool: An Example

PART III. SECOND LEG OF THE STRATEGY
RIGGING THE EAST POOL
- Conservative Investments: Are There Any?
- Can We Predict The Future?
- Diversification Protects You Against An Uncertain Future
- Setting Up The East Pool: An Example
- The East Pool Technique: Why Does It Work?

PART IV. THIRD LEG OF THE STRATEGY
SPECULATING WITH THE WEST POOL
- How To Create The West Pool
- What To Do With The Money In The West Pool
- Should You Have A West Pool At All?
- Rules Of The Wild West
- No One Can Guarantee Success When You Speculate

PART V. PUTTING IT ALL TOGETHER
"THE COMPLEAT STRATEGIST"

CHAPTER 4: Investing In Real Estate 83

INTRODUCTION
SETTING THE SCENE
- Advantages And Disadvantages Of Real Estate
- Disadvantages
- Advantages
- Investment Objectives

HOW TO FIND IT AND WHAT TO DO WITH IT
- Where To Look And What To Look For
- How Much To Pay
- Leveraging
- Timing
- Sources of Financing
- Tax Issues

GOING IT ALONE OR WITH OTHERS
- Forms Of Group Investing

SPECIFIC TYPES OF REAL ESTATE OPPORTUNITIES

CHAPTER 5: Mutual Funds 111

INTRODUCTION
INVESTING IN MUTUAL FUNDS
- Advantages
- Disadvantages
- Management Fees And Sales Charges
- The Front-End Load
- Hidden Loads And Rear-End Loads

MUTUAL FUNDS AND YOUR RRSP
GETTING OUT OF YOUR RRSP "TAX FREE"
LEVERAGING

SAVING FOR A CHILD'S EDUCATION
BOND, MORTGAGE AND INCOME FUNDS
DIVIDEND FUNDS
UNSCRUPULOUS SALES PRACTICES
NINE TIPS ON BUYING MUTUAL FUNDS

CHAPTER 6: Low-Risk Investing 121
INTRODUCTION
AVOID LOSING MONEY
LONG-TERM INVESTING
  • Diversify
  • Variability
  • Risk
  • Reward
MUTUAL FUND PORTFOLIOS
  • Performance
  • ChartLists
SUMMARY

CHAPTER 7: Investing For Growth 131
INTRODUCTION
TREASURY BILLS
INCREASING YOUR INVESTMENT INCOME
  • Bonds
  • Mortgage-Backed Securities
  • Preferred Shares
  • Convertible Preferreds and Convertible Debentures
GROWTH OF CAPITAL
  • Mutual Funds
  • Building A Stock Portfolio
  • New Issues
  • Foreign Investing
  • Special Situations
YOU AND YOUR BROKER

CHAPTER 8: Legal Aids 143
INTRODUCTION
FAMILY LAW
REAL ESTATE
STARTING UP A SMALL BUSINESS
ESTATE AND WILL PLANNING
A COLLECTION OF TAX TIPS
  • Evasion Or Avoidance
  • Pay Tax On Time
  • What To Do If You Are Reassessed
  • Partners And Proprietors
  • Reduce Tax
  • Every Parent Can Income Split
  • Planning For Tax Reform

CHAPTER 9: Consumer Law 155
INTRODUCTION
CONTRACT LAW
  • Mutual Agreement
  • Consideration Or A Seal
  • Capacity To Contract
  • Lawful Subject Matter
  • Intention To Create Binding Legal Relations

SOME SPECIAL TYPES OF CONTRACTS
- Personal Guarantees
- What Is A Personal Guarantee?
- Guarantor's Rights And Obligations
- Practical Considerations
- Insurance Contracts

SUGGESTIONS BEFORE YOU SIGN
PURCHASING GOODS AND SERVICES
- Implied Terms In A Contract Of Sale
- Buying A Car And Getting It Repaired
- Buying A Car
- Manufacturers' Warranties
- Repairing Your Car
- Buying On Credit
- What If You Can't Pay?

PROTECTION FOR THE CONSUMER
- Door-To-Door Sales
- Unsolicited Goods And Credit Cards
- Misleading Advertising
- What Types Of Advertising Are Misleading?
- What Remedies Are Available?

HOW TO MAKE YOUR COMPLAINT
- The Phone Call Or Personal Visit
- Sending A Letter
- Third Party Assistance
- Taking Legal Action
- Choosing A Lawyer
- Is A Specialist Needed?
- How Much Will A Lawyer Cost?

CHAPTER 10: Your Own Home-Based Business 173

INTRODUCTION
WHO ME?
WHAT KIND OF BUSINESS TO START?
THE BUSINESS PLAN
- Type
- Business Name
- Ownership
- Business Location
- Products/Services Offered
- Price
- Who Buys Your Product/Service?
- Competitors
- Cash Or Credit
- Bank Account
- Business Cards And Stationery
- Telephone
- Setting Up The Office
- Marketing
- How Much Money?
- Credit Ratings
- Income Tax
- Finding Experts
- Resources

APPENDIX 189

About the Authors

The Contributing Authors to this book are also contributors to *Canadian MoneySaver*. Each writer is considered an expert on his/her topic. The contributors are: Dale Ennis, Don Zinyk, Chuck Chakrapani, Keith Laushway, Bill McLeod, Don Pooley, Nancy Foster, Karen Selick, Terry Wagar and Lynn Anderson.

Dale Ennis is the publishing editor and founder of *Canadian MoneySaver*. He is responsible for publishing other financial periodicals and books for Canadian Money Saver Inc. As an extension of this information service, he also conducts money management seminars throughout Canada. *Canadian MoneySaver*, P.O. Box 370, Bath, Ontario K0H 1G0 (613) 352-7448.

Don Zinyk is a partner in Thorne Ernst & Whinney's Edmonton office, dealing primarily with independent business clients, and personal financial and taxation planning matters. Don contributed a business article to the first edition of this book. Thorne Ernst & Whinney, 3000 Canadian Commercial Bank Tower, Edmonton Centre West, 10104-103 Avenue, Edmonton, Alberta T5J 3V8 (403) 425-0240.

Dr. Chuck Chakrapani has authored several books on investing, such as: *Financial Freedom on $5 a Day, Best Ways to Make Money* and *Gold: A Guide to Investment Profits*. Chuck is the editor of *Money Digest* and chairman of Investors Association of Canada. I.A.C., P.O. Box 370, Bath, Ontario K0H 1G0 (613) 352-7448.

Keith Laushway, lawyer, works as a senior manager in the tax department of Peat Marwick, a firm of chartered accountants with the Canadian head office in Toronto. Keith also teaches at the University of Toronto. As well he has written a number of articles on various subjects. Peat Marwick, Commerce Court West, Toronto, Ontario M5L 1B2 (416) 863-3767.

Tax Shelters and *Shoppers' Guide to Canadian Life In-*

surance Policies and Prices are two consumer books written by Bill McLeod. Bill teaches personal finance and business courses at Cambrian College in Sudbury, Ontario. Bill McLeod, 15 Eden Point Drive, Sudbury, Ontario P3E 4V6 (705) 522-3858.

Don Pooley has been invited to describe his financial planning methods to audiences in every major city in Canada and at other international sites. His articles have been published in *CA Magazine*, the *Financial Post* and the *Financial Times*. Don Pooley, 1849 West 35th Avenue, Vancouver, British Columbia V6M 1H5 (604) 261-2194.

Nancy Foster is with Richardson Greenshields of Canada. She is recognized as a dynamic speaker and participates in various seminars and workshops. Richardson Greenshields, 44 Princess Street, Kingston, Ontario K7L 4V8 (613) 549-6370.

Karen Selick is a practising lawyer who specializes in family and commercial law, wills and estates. She has been a contributor to *Financial Post, Financial Times* and *Canadian MoneySaver*. Reynolds, Hunter, 183 Front Street, Box 1327 Belleville, Ontario K8N 5J7 (613) 966-3031.

Terry Wagar's home is usually in Halifax, Nova Scotia. However, a leave of absence from St. Mary's University this year permits him to complete his Ph.D. outside Canada. Terry is a legal expert on financial matters. Terry Wagar, LL.B, MBA, MIR, P.O. Box 370, Bath, Ontario K0H 1G0 (613) 352-7448.

Lynn Anderson is a home-based business advocate and entrepreneur. She has established a non-profit association for business people in the Ottawa region. Lynn conducts numerous seminars for starting your own business and keeping it profitable. A.S.A.P., 20 Hobart Crescent, Nepean, Ontario K2H 5S4 (613) 726-0485.

Preface

Our *Guide To Making Money* has been written to help the "ordinary" Canadian understand and make sense out of money matters s/he encounters everyday. We believe that you are the best person to help yourself become your own money expert. You can become financially secure without expending a great deal of time or effort. The way to financial security is not hard to learn.

Guide To Making Money takes you through an easy-to-understand step-by-step money management program which will lead you to financial success. The program is designed to help beginners by evaluating their current financial position, and then taking them through to the later stages of investing. Those who already know the basics may plug into the program at their own stage of knowledge and development. We will also outline how you can keep your program alive on a long-term basis.

You will be shown how to set short-term and long-term financial goals, and how your present financial situation can be altered, if necessary, to meet these goals more easily. Simple elementary money facts are explained through numerous examples, charts and graphs. These principles will demonstrate how you can spend or invest your money to maximize its earning power. We'll also show you how to locate "found" money — money that is not being used to its best and most profitable advantage.

Virtually anyone can achieve a comfortable level of financial security. A number of spending patterns and investment techniques will be discussed in detail so that you can identify which route is best for you. For example, getting rid of personal debt, buying a home, and later beginning an investment program in a logical order will create wealth. Our RIGging strategy outlines how to get rich ... slowly. You won't find any risky or get-rich-quick schemes detailed here — only proven techniques.

This book provides all the details that are essential for you to know to use your money smartly. We also show you how to chart the tax consequences of your decisions so that you are able to make sound selections before you invest.

You may save yourself hundreds of dollars before signing a contract or visiting a lawyer by first consulting our chapter on legal matters. If you wish to make money in a business of your own, we include the information you'll need to start a part-time or full-time business.

Our authors are all highly respected individuals who have gained expertise in their respective fields. Their advice will help you make your money grow. If we haven't covered everything you want to know in this book, or if you still have unanswered questions when you are finished reading, you can contact the authors directly through the provided addresses.

Financial security comes from the on-going awareness of money development and the monitoring of your own personal cash flow. *Guide To Making Money* will give you that extra edge by helping you understand, in easy-to-read clear language, all the essential ingredients for your success.

I wish you the best —

Dale Ennis

CHAPTER 1

PERSONAL MONEY MANAGEMENT

By Dale Ennis

INTRODUCTION

A recent Canadian study has revealed that only 1 in 10 retired people can carry his/her preretirement lifestyle into his/her retirement years. And socio-economic level has little bearing on this situation.

A Woods Gordon report, *Tomorrow's Customers*, states that "by 2006, there will be 25% more dependents over 65 than in 1986 but over 25% fewer young dependents under 17. The increase in older dependents will probably call for a reassessment of existing government pension and medical plans which may be strained by the burden of so many more retired people in the decades to come. Private pension plans, registered retirement savings plans and other investment vehicles are being looked to as important ingredients in a financially comfortable retirement."

Unfortunately, in the past few years many Canadians have witnessed salary increments which may only keep up with inflation. Since 1982 the Canada Pension Plan premiums (see appendix) and\Unemployment Insurance contributions have increased at a rate\greater than the inflation rate.

Federal tax changes have also decreased our take-home pay. The child tax credit system, the federal tax reduction, the standard medical/charitable deduction, and the maximum employment expense deduction have all been altered or eliminated (for 1988) to our detriment. And Provincial income tax rates continue to increase. Refer to the appendix for a breakdown of these changes.

These reasons are a few of the causes for our shrinking disposable incomes. In general most of us are faced with the Law of Diminishing Returns — usually after a few years of employment our financial peak is experienced. As stated earlier, few of us have salary increments which allow us to surpass or even equal the various eroding factors of our dollars and the buying power of those dollars. Thus, you fall farther and farther behind unless you decide to take action. The income curve illustrates our dilemma.

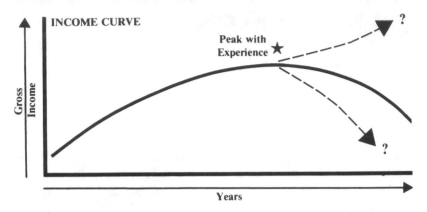

Many Canadian experts have serious doubts that Old Age Security (O.A.S.) will remain a universal program, fully indexed, especially for those individuals presently under 50 years of age. There is even doubt that the Canada Pension Plan will be available for baby boomers. The Woods Gordon report appears to be more proof of these concerns.

What can you expect from your private pension plan(s)? Fortunately, major revisions are taking place and portability is being established. It is essential that you ask your personnel advisor about your financial position for the future. Some pensions are fully indexed (e.g., government), but most company pensions are quite inadequate for support. And remember that if you take early retirement your pension will be reduced (integrated) at 65 when Canada Pension is received. For an indepth reading of the pension plan regulations, an excellent book, *Looking After the Future*, may be consulted.

Today as never before you can readily recognize the need to begin retirement and financial planning as early as possible. A Canadian university professor's study found that retirement planning is becoming more common, but in many cases, it is too little too late. Starting the plan for retirement earlier can significantly improve your financial picture during retirement. Advanced planning is essential, particularly financial planning, because financial status has a major impact on all aspects of well-being.

An extremely high percentage of Canadians purchase financial vehicles through default when they are "in season", and not necessarily at the best time, when they fit well into a plan. A Stanford study found that purchases were completed for the following reasons: 94% purchased due to the charisma of the salesperson (by default), 5% as a portfolio decision, and only 1% for a long-range strategic plan.

Your financial plan must be initiated at a strategic level — considered from the wide perspective of what you want out of life, not from the narrow perspective of the benefits of one product. Once you have identified this perspective (or overall plan) progress can be made. Goals will be attained, and the chance of stress and other associated illnesses will be lessened. The "Happiness Chart" will help us focus on this simple concept.

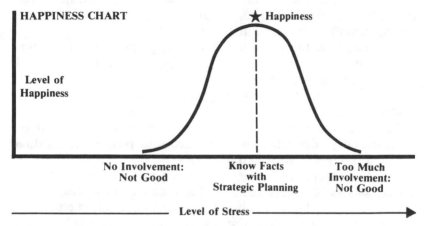

HAPPINESS CHART

★ Happiness

Level of
Happiness

No Involvement:	Know Facts	Too Much
Not Good	with	Involvement:
	Strategic Planning	Not Good

———— Level of Stress ————▶

— Stress increases if people worry about finances.
— No investment plan leads to worry.

With no planning it is quite difficult to identify your progress (or digression). Stress may be increased, as there is little feeling of accomplishment. Therefore it is imperative that we develop a personal plan and keep current with the ever-changing strategies available to us (keep current by sending for a free copy of the *MoneySaver* as listed at the end of this chapter). We can carry out this technique by understanding what is available and setting up an overall plan.

YOUR FINANCIAL PLAN

"People don't plan to fail — they simply fail to plan." Some experts have suggested that you spend an amount of time on money management equal to your marginal tax rate! If your marginal tax rate is 20%, it means that you should use 20% of your "free" time for personal money management.

Let's examine the various phases of this planning process.

Phase One: Net Worth

The first step, the net worth statement, is really an inventory of your current financial position. Your statement lists your assets and your liabilities or debts. Your assets minus your liabilities produces your family's net worth.

Your assets include such items as your house, car, boat, furniture, clothing, cash investments and Registered Retirement Savings Plans. Your liabilities or debts may include your mortgage, money owed on a car or credit card, investment loans, income taxes and outstanding bills.

To determine the value of your belongings, you could consider their cash value if you sold them. Some investments should be evaluated at after-tax rates.

This net worth statement lets you find out exactly where you stand. It shows you where you spend your money, and gives you an indication of what you might expect, financially, if you faced an emergency. Your study will enhance your position to set up a personal budget if you need to do so.

Your net worth statement will be of value to your family. Later, as you feel more comfortable with this task and/or feel the need to develop individual family member statements, you could extend this practice. For a sample chart please refer to the appendix. An annual net worth excercise will help you identify your progress. Hopefully you will recognize a positive annual growth which you could graph for visual awareness.

Most financial institutions will give you complimentary net worth forms. A rather comprehensive booklet with net worth, budget and objective forms is available free from the Information Centre, Canadian Life and Health Insurance Association. Call toll free: 1-800-268-8099. (A great number of other insurance booklets are also provided free of charge.)

Phase Two: Goal Setting

Where would you like to be sitting financially five years from now? How about ten? While budgeting is very important to your financial future, by itself it's just not enough. If you'd really like to accomplish something spectacular — or even just retire above the poverty line — you'll do so much better if you set specific financial goals for yourself and your family.

Goal setting is very "in" these days, and you've probably dabbled in a few yourself. Perhaps you've planned a fitness routine towards a goal of eventually running a marathon, or are just trying to eat healthier foods from now on. Goals can be tough and extremely challenging, or simple and relatively easy, but they have one very vital thing in common — they help us focus our energies on what we would like to achieve. Without goals of any kind, many people tend to wander through life, hoping that what they would like to see happen, does.

But once you set a goal for yourself, you can actually see it coming true as you work towards it. Goals create energy, because all of a sudden you know exactly where you're going, and precisely what you need to do to get there. And seeing tangible results helps to keep you psyched up.

"Goals add direction," states Peter Volpe, the Toronto manager of financial services for Royal Trust, "but only if you set specific goals in relation to your personal values and needs. A clearly defined goal can be budgeted for and worked towards, but a vague target makes it difficult to do anything specific."

"Too many people don't have the vaguest idea where their money goes, or what they should be doing with it," feels Debbi Lockie, partner in Minpar Consultants. "And yet everybody has something he wants — a trip, a new car, whatever. But none of these things can have any reality until you make a plan. With a good plan, you can say here is what I can do."

"I have found that people who have definite financial plans achieve more than those who don't because they are able to dovetail their annual cash flow predictions to their annual cash requirements," says Graeme Goebelle, of the Chartered Accountants firm of Goebelle, MacAdam and Alexander in Georgetown, Ontario. "You have to put special emphasis on the areas where there are variances so that you can sort them out. The prime concern of financial management is utilitarian rather than philosophical, and it is responsible for matching your needs with your resources."

Getting Started. "The hardest part is sitting down and actually making your goals," says Kim Ball, seminar manager for the Women's Financial Planning Center in Toronto. "Once the goals are in place, you'll find that they will practically run themselves."

The key to controlling your financial future is deciding your goals, and then tailoring a specific plan to fit your own particular circumstances. So start by having a good talk with your spouse, your whole family, and yourself."

Where are you now, financially? What is the state of your family's comfort and security? What would you seriously like to accomplish over the next few years, and what sort of capital do you need to do it? And last but certainly not least, what sort of retirement would you like to have?

Once you've clearly decided what is really important to you, then you can start formulating your goals. All you need is a few pieces of paper or a small notebook. Writing down your plans makes them real, and you'll find it easier to go over them for encouragement. But just because they're written down, does not mean that they're carved in stone. A good, workable financial goals program is flexible and realistic — it changes easily as your circumstances change.

"The purpose of accumulating money is to give yourself choices," states Kim Ball, "so you should never feel trapped by your goals. They should be reviewed every six months or every year, and changed according to what has happened in your life."

"It's most important to be realistic when setting your financial goals, otherwise you may get discouraged too easily. "Most people first come for financial advice because they're frustrated with their financial position, and have a real desire to do better for a specific reason," says Peter Volpe. "Goals should ideally be both realistic and flexible, or else they can be frustrating too, and you'll quickly abandon them."

In other words, it's lovely to dream about living in a million dollar penthouse condo someday, but it cannot be a tangible goal if you're presently making only $10,000 a year. Why not start with the goal of training for a new job or upgrading your skills so you can double your salary in the next few years?

Short-term Goals. The first goals you should consider are those you can achieve within the next couple of years. Where you should start depends on your current financial situation.

Most financial planners feel that your wisest first step — in any financial program — is setting up an emergency fund. Since you never know when you might fall ill or lose your job, preparing for these possibilities should be your first priority. People who are unprepared can, in the event of a financial catastrophe, dig themselves into deep debt or even bankruptcy, from which they may never truly recover.

"You should never plan on actually using your emergency fund," says Wood Gundy Account Executive Toby Condliffe, "but just having some money available to you in case of financial emergency is extremely important." Some people, of course, need more on reserve than others. Someone with a large family and a stiff mortgage will need much more than a single person who rents a small apartment. But however much you need, you should think about having about six months' worth of money available to you.

"Life just doesn't run smoothly," says Debbi Lockie, "and you never know what will happen. I recommend that everybody have some money put aside in the event of an emergency, and I am a big fan of Canada Savings Bonds for this purpose. They're instantly cashable, and yet just inaccessible enough so that you won't run to them every time you run out of money at the end of the month."

Toby Condliffe stresses that, although you do need some emergency money, it doesn't have to be your money.

"If you have trouble saving enough money, consider simply opening up a line of credit at your bank. It costs you absolutely nothing if you don't use it, and if you do, works just like an instant loan. It's like money in the bank!

If your own bank won't extend a line of credit to you, shop around, as all banks have different criteria. You can also shop around for the best interest rate — in any case, you'll find it significantly less than your credit card or even a consumer loan.

Your second major short-term goal should be to reduce your debts. "You must get control of your spending habits, or there's really no point in making goals," feels Lockie. She suggests that you get current with your credit cards first, as this debt is the most costly to carry (as high as 28% on some department store cards). "Bill consolidation loans work wonders when you have a lot of expensive credit card debts," Lockie continued. "If you're paying out $200-300 a month on those charge cards, a loan will reduce that amount — but you should put back the money saved in interest towards paying off that debt, so that you can pay it back faster. "And, of course," she concluded, "stop using those credit cards!"

After your cards, you should work towards paying off any consumer loans you may have — perhaps for your car. And thirdly, it should be in your plans to reduce your mortgage as much as you can as early as you can.

Although you may long to buy gold or dabble in stocks, you'll end up much healthier financially in the long run if you see to these two short-term goals first. Once you are covered in the event of emergency and reasonably out of debt (except for your mortgage), then you can think of investing safely.

Medium-range Goals. Things that you can accomplish within the next five or so years can make the most exciting goals. They're not so distant that they're impossible to see, just tantalizingly far enough away to keep us highly motivated. These will be the most personalized, as each one of us dreams his own dream.

"You can't really answer any questions about spending your money over the long run until you have your specific goals listed in a priority sequence," states Volpe, "and this gives you a good starting point. Otherwise, you may lose your enthusiasm entirely. You need this structure to build upon."

If you're discussing starting a family within the next few years, you might want to set a goal to save enough money to allow one parent to quit work to stay home with the child for the first couple of years. If you already have young children, one of the most valuable goals you can set is to be sure that there's enough money available for college or university when it's needed.

But you should look into educational plans carefully, warns Tony De Thomasis, chartered financial planner with Money Rates & Answers. Some old-style funds tie up your money, and the interest is lost if your child doesn't go on to college or university. "Two excellent plans are the various stock broker education funds for the experienced investor, or the new Bolton Tremblay Education Fund for someone who wants to use a professional fund manager," De Thomasis explained. "But any good fund is better than just putting money into a savings account. The more inaccessible your money is, the less likely you are to dip into it for some other purpose."

Other medium-range goals might be to move into a house within the next five-to-ten years, and to work on getting together a down payment or perhaps you'd like to take a cruise. Or maybe you can see a luxury car or even a boat in your future.

Mid-range goals, more than any others, depend on exactly what is important to you, and this is why it's so vital to really think about what you want to achieve in your life. Tony De Thomasis suggests bringing the whole family in on this discussion. "Cash flow — money that can be spent today — is more important to some people than saving for something in the future. If, for example, your family really doesn't mind living in an apartment, there's no need to scrimp and save for a home. It's good to know yourself."

"You make financial plans ultimately to enhance your

lifestyle," Volpe said. "You have to think of what you want to do with your life now, and not compromise all of your enjoyment today for your future. You can attain it all with the proper blending of your desires. Both now and your retirement are important."

Long-term goals. If you should compare your goals with a neighbour, you'll probably find that your long-term goals are quite similar. You may want a bigger home, a fabulous trip around the world, a home in Florida, or it may be important to you to leave a large estate to your children. Most likely, you'll also want a very secure and comfortable retirement — and maybe even an early one.

There are many ways to save for the distant future, and any financial planner can steer you in the right direction for your situation. What you should decide, of course, depends on your age now. Your plans will be different if you're twenty rather than fifty.

But everyone agrees that the RRSPs are one of the best deals going. Tony De Thomasis likes them so much, in fact, that he recommends that you have three of them! Since no one can predict the future, there's no way to ensure the success of any one vehicle. So he suggests you have one plan at a guaranteed rate (for utmost safety), one that uses stocks or investment funds (which might perform spectacularly), and one to fight inflation with gold or real estate (who knows how well they might do!).

Remember that RRSPs certainly don't have to be kept until you're 65. They make excellent savings vehicles for any purpose at all, and can be as easily collapsed for your three-month trip to the Orient as they can for your retirement.

Kim Ball suggests starting your savings the easy way, by having your bank automatically debit 5% of every check you deposit, and placing it into a separate account. (This is assuming that 5% is already going to a pension fund. If you have no pension fund, save 10% from every check.) Whenever you accumulate a reasonable amount, move the money into something that will pay more interest. She also likes savings bonds, but feels that GICs are too inflexible. "You should be free to move your money around any time you wish," she said, "to get the best rate of return. And of course you can add money to your RRSP anytime during the year, not only in February."

Keeping On Track. Even the most thought-out goals will be of no use to you if you don't follow through on them, so financial experts all agree that you should allow for some kind of reward along the way. "Living frugally has no attraction over the long run, no matter what you're saving for," says Kim Ball, "so you should allow yourself occasional treats. I recommend things like a dinner out after each $100 saved, or a little trip to Florida after each $5,000 put away. You'll be amazed how painless it becomes to save when you have this kind of incentive!"

"Many goals have built-in rewards," points out Debbi Lockie. "If you've saved three years for a fur coat, then you have the fur coat! That is a reward in itself. But if you need something beyond that — or if you're saving for something intangible — consider an incentive like blowing $100 on anything you wish each time you reach your six-month savings goal."

Of course the best way to keep on track is to review your written goals frequently — even every Monday morning. When you actually are reminded often where you're headed, and can actually see the progress you're making, it keeps your enthusiasm high. In other words, the better you do, the better you'll want to do.

But of course it can be difficult to stay on the straight and narrow at times. "You'll find that the closer you get to your goals, the easier it will be to discipline yourself," says Lockie. "But don't let little slips here and there along the way cause you to scrap the whole project.

"It's like when you're on a diet. Don't berate yourself when you fall off the wagon — just jump right back on and keep going!"

Should You Consult A Financial Planner? Once your goals have been set, you might want to consider seeking the advice of a financial planner. There are just so many ways to "save" money these days that it would take a genius to figure them all out.

"You should never sacrifice liquidity for income," Toby Condliffe feels. "You should set up your financial program so that you can always change your mind." He recommends Canada Savings Bonds as about the best thing you can do with money that you don't have in specific plans. They earn more than savings accounts, and yet can be cashed in with no trouble or waiting if you need the money. He prefers them to savings vehicles like GICs, which, as he said, should only be used by people who need the comfort of knowing that their money is safe and sound in the bank. "You can do better elsewhere," he says.

De Thomasis also points out that preferred shares or investment funds can offer the average person high dividends and low risk. And like the other investment programs, money in these forms is just inaccessible enough that you'll probably leave it alone.

But what if you have a bit of the gambler in you? Many financial planners feel that you can never become really wealthy unless you are willing to take a few risks. But how can this fit into your set of goals?

"I recommend that you don't dabble in any high-risk ventures — stocks, gold, or real estate — until you have a cushion of at least $10,000-$15,000 in easily-accessible (liquid) form, like savings bonds," De Thomasis said. "Then, when your cash flow can afford it — go for it!"

Now that you agree on the need for goal setting, here are the guidelines for completing phase two.

Based on your net worth, you and your family members can set realistic objectives in the financial sphere. Since career, personal and educational goals are so interwined with financial objectives, all areas of interest should be examined.

Goals should be established for various terms. It is advisable to consider the short term (up to one year), the medium term (one to five years), and the long term (five to ten years). All goals should be committed to paper for immediate and long-term reference. Each goal should be specific — i.e., "to save $1000 annually" rather than "to save money". Goals should be measurable so that you may determine your ability to reach them. Naturally, these goals should be reasonably attainable — e.g., to save $500 annually if $1000 is improbable.

Each family member should set his/her personal goals independent of other members. Once this task is completed, all members should develop a family objective guide together. Through this consensus approach, everyone will recognize the need and importance for sharing his individual concerns. A greater commitment for the family goals will result from this discussion. This give-and-take approach may also be instrumental in starting family counselling meetings for future financial interests.

A single page may be set up based on the outline provided in the appendix. This guide should be used individually before the family objectives are committed to paper.

Phase Three: Cash Flow Forecasting

A cash flow forecast is a process designed to help you identify your financial needs over a specific period of time. You project your income(s) and expenses by estimating the amounts that relate to the time period which you have selected. Usually the forecast is struck on a monthly basis over a twelve-month period.

Therefore, forecasting is the logical forerunner of intelligent budgeting (which is planned to meet certain financial goals in a relatively short period of time). A cash flow forecast may be set up using the following outline:

- Buy paper divided into columns. The first column describes each item. Subsequent columns are used for each time period (e.g., weeks or months).
- Begin with the word "incomes" at the top of the description column and list your source(s) of money. Start with the familar incomes for each period. Estimate less predictable incomes (interest, gratuities, etc.).
- By adding each column, you determine the total income(s) for each period.
- Now write the word "expenses" in the description column. Begin with your fixed cost, such as the mortgage, rent or grocery bill. Then estimate the variable costs such as entertainment and vacations.
- By adding each column you determine the total expenses for each time period.
- Subtract the expenses from the income(s) to calculate your net cash flow.
- "Cash at start" is the amount of money you had on hand at the beginning of this forecast period. This money may be held in a bank account so that all transactions conveniently flow through it.
- If the net flow is positive (as November's $290) in the following chart, you add it to the cash at start. If negative (as December's $550) in the following chart, you subtract it from the cash at start.
- The new total indicates your cash position at the end of the time period. This amount is carried forward to the "cash at start" for the next period.
- Continue this pattern until your cash flow forecast is complete. Remember, you select the time period which is best suited for you.

The following chart will serve to demonstrate an example of a cash flow forecast:

Incomes:	November	December	January	October
Net Salary	$1,900	$1,900	$2,000 (raise)	$2,000
Interest	$ 75	$ 75	$ 85	$ 85
TOTAL	$1,975	$1,975	$2,085	$2,085
Expenses:				
Mortgage	$ 650	$ 650	$ 650	$ 650
Car Payments	$ 125	$ 125	$ 125	$ 125
Car Insurance	$ 160			$ 160
Food	$ 300	$ 300	$ 300	$ 350
Entertainment	$ 100	$ 100	100	$ 100
Renovations			$ 500	
Vacation		$1,000		
Other	$ 350	$ 350	$ 350	$ 400
TOTAL	$1,685	$2,525	$2,025	$1,735
Net Cash Flow	$ 290	$ (550) (negative)	$ 60	$ 350
Cash at Start	$ 750	$1,040	$ 490	$ 890
New Total	$1,040	$ 490	$ 550	$1,240

It is evident that this hypothetical family will probably have sufficient funds to meet its needs over this twelve-month period. (Emergency and investment monies are held in other accounts.) This forecast has permitted family members to look into the financial future and ease their possible worry concerning their money needs. If a negative cash flow is discovered by this exercise, the necessary adjustment can be made long before the stressful situation is encountered. This awareness prevents last-minute adjustments and the accompanying family and financial pressures.

If you are unaccustomed to completing a regular monthly budget, you may need to follow a budgeting system for a while before attempting the cash flow forecast. As you have noticed, you require some budgeting practice on a short-term basis before a long-term plan can be implemented.

Phase Four: Budgeting

A personal financial plan (budget) is the only certain way to reach your money goals. This income and expense statement enables you to use your income to its best advantage. This analysis of how you spend your money clearly shows you the allocation of your dollars each month. With a well-thought-out plan, a portion of your income (savings) is allocated to various forms of investment.

Construct your plan so that it encourages investing each month with money set aside for this purpose — not with whatever is left over. This means that you pay yourself first.

Establish a regular savings plan. Initially you may save only two or three percent of your net (take-home pay) income. As you become accustomed to this practice, increase this savings when it is convenient to do so. A realistic goal for savings would vary between 5 and 10% of your net income. The key point here is that the savings must be taken out of expenses before other deductions. Our sample budget, in the appendix, has the savings deduction first.

One brief note concerning incomes. Your monthly take-home wage is after deductions such as union fees, Unemployment Insurance Commission premiums, Canada Pension Plan contributions and income tax. However, income should also include possible commissions, gifts, profits from sales, rental and investment income.

Some expenses are fixed/regular and therefore relatively easy to calculate — rent/mortgage, taxes, loans, etc. Many flexible expenses are determined by our seasons — heating, recreation, home improvements, etc. These irregular expenses will require a "guesstimate" in some cases. Your past experience with these expenditures will be your best guide for future calculations. As you become a seasoned budgeter you will recognize the patterns of your expenses.

The following suggestions may be useful to you:
- One method to help you discipline yourself to budget properly is to use a form of payroll deduction. Automatic withdrawals at work or at your banking institution may make it easier for you to save.
- Try to purchase for your needs before your wants. Frivolously spending for items you want may develop poor money management habits.
- It may be necessary to prepare for lifestyle changes, for example, entertaining at home rather than at restaurants. What would happen if one regular salary was eliminated?
- If you do not have sufficient money for your budget, you may have to cut back on expenses, take a part-time job, or set more realistic goals.
- You can become budget-minded, prevent impulsive buying and cut back use (and abuse) of your credit card.

- The provincial Association of Credit Counselling Services provides complementary material as well as personal counselling service.
- Budgeting workbooks are available free through several financial institutions like The Royal Bank, and through the provincial Consumer and Commercial Affairs offices.
- Copy our sample budget sheet from the appendix. Enlarge it. Start filling it out today.

Now that you have established your personal financial position, you are ready to begin examining how to use your money, how to invest your savings, and how to plan for your future retirement. This next section will present some basic yet crucial concepts you should understand before advancing to these stages of investing.

FINANCIAL CONCEPTS

Three main objectives of your personal financial plan are to protect what you have, to accumulate money, and to retire in relative comfort. Therefore it is essential that you identify the financial strategies and vehicles which will permit you to achieve these objectives. If you become aware of various financial concepts and investment strategies, you are well on your way to financial security.

Inflation

Inflation is the ever decreasing power of your dollar. The secret is not to ignore inflation, but to understand its effects in order to minimize its impact.

You should know that everyone does not share the same inflation level. If it is stated that our national inflation rate is five percent, thousands of Canadians will actually experience an inflation rate significantly above or below this reported figure. Why?

The inflation rate is based on the Consumer Price Index (CPI). The CPI is composed of the level of prices of various goods and services that the average Canadian family reportedly purchases. This composition tends to be constant and unchanging (revised every ten years with the census). Each item is weighted at a different percentage. For example, housing, food and transportation (including energy) are weighted more heavily than other components by Statistics Canada. Therefore, if you spend a higher than average number of dollars on food, your inflation rate will actually be proportionately higher than the national average. Other factors besides spending patterns will effect this rate. For example, you may have an inflation rate of 4.6%, but move to Toronto and it will increase to 6.3%!

The applicability of the CPI to the individual is rather low. However, it does provide a general indicator for our personal inflation rate. And since you are reading this book, it is probably safe to say that your inflation rate is higher than the national average.

Let's examine some specific examples to recognize how our dollar can shrink due to the effects of inflation. The following inflation equivalent chart illustrates the effect of low inflation on today's buying power of only $1,000:

INFLATION EQUIVALENTS OF $1,000

Years	5%	7-1/2%	10%
1	$1,050	$1,075	$ 1,100
5	$1,267	$1,436	$ 1,611
10	$1,629	$2,061	$ 2,594
15	$2,079	$2,959	$ 4,177
20	$2,653	$4,248	$ 6,728
25	$3,386	$6,098	$10,835

This chart shows you that in only five years of 5% inflation, you will need $1,267 to purchase goods that your $1,000 will buy today.

Two practical examples of the eroding power of inflation can be seen in the following chart:

ANNUAL INFLATION

Rate	Item	Cost Now	15 yrs.	20 yrs.	25 yrs.
7-1/2%	Groceries	$ 100	$ 296	$ 425	$ 610
7-1/2%	House Prices	$59,000	$174,500	$250,000	$359,000
10%	House Prices	$59,000	$246,400	$396,900	$639,200

If you wish to purchase a home in 15 years which today is valued at $59,000, you will need $174,500 (59 x $2,959) at only a 7-1/2% inflation rate! That means that you will purchase the same home in 15 years at this inflated price simply because of the inflation rate. If real estate prices also go up, your cost will be even higher.

Our last inflation-related chart reveals the minimum investment return you must receive to maintain your net worth. The marginal tax rates are based on the proposed 1988 federal rates. The figures for marginal tax rate (MTR) are for illustrative purposes only. A more detailed explanation for calculating your positon is found later in this chapter.

ASSUMED RATE OF INFLATION

		5%	6%	10%	12%
Federal Rate (1988) + Provincial Rate = MTR		Breakeven Rate of Return*			
17.0% (up to $27,500)	25%	6.7	8.0	13.3	16.0
26.0% (up to $55,000)	40%	8.3	10.0	16.7	20.0
29.0% (over $55,000)	45%	9.1	10.9	18.2	21.8

* Investment income deductions eliminated for 1988.

Now you can readily recognize the need to constantly monitor your inflation rate for spending and investment purposes. A more complete inflation/interest table has been placed in our appendix for specific calculations.

Interest

One of the world's richest men was once asked what he thought was "The Eighth Wonder of the World". He quickly responded "compounding".

When you are quoted a rate for a loan or mortgage, the bank is quoting the nominal rate, not the real rate. The nominal rate consists of two components: the real rate and the inflation component. The real rate is the bank's profit. The cost of money increases as inflation does and is the inflation component. The banks charge for an anticipated inflation change.

Please consider this extreme example. You are offered a job for 30 days. You may work for $100 a day or you may work for one cent the first day and allow your pay to double from the previous day on each succeeding day. Which offer do you select?

It is quite obvious which offer you will accept if you know the facts. However, it is surprising how few people use the compounding effect of money in their daily lives.

Compounding is the process of reinvesting the income from the original investment and in turn reinvesting the yield of the total accumulating investment. Simply put, it means that you earn interest on interest.

The following table will illustrate the effects of compounding on nominal rates:

MAGIC OF COMPOUNDING

Day	$100/Day	The 1¢ Offer
1	$100.00	.01
2	100.00	.02
3	100.00	.04
4	100.00	.08
5	100.00	.16
6	100.00	.32
7	100.00	.64
8	100.00	1.28
9	100.00	2.56
10	100.00	5.12
11	100.00	10.24
12	100.00	20.48
13	100.00	40.96
14	100.00	81.92
15	100.00	163.84
16	100.00	327.68
17	100.00	655.36
18	100.00	1,310.72
19	100.00	2,621.44
20	100.00	5,242.88
21	100.00	10,485.76
22	100.00	20,971.52
23	100.00	41,943.04
24	100.00	83,886.08
25	100.00	167,772.16
26	100.00	335,544.32
27	100.00	671,088.64
28	100.00	1,342,177.28
29	100.00	2,684,354.56
30	100.00	5,368,709.12
	Total $3,000.00	Total $10,737,418.23

EFFECTIVE ANNUAL RATE

Nominal Rate	Annual Compounding	Semi-Annual Compounding	Monthly Compounding	Daily Compounding
9.00%	9.0000	9.2025	9.3807	9.4162
9.25%	9.2500	9.4639	9.6524	9.6900
9.50%	9.5000	9.7256	9.9248	9.9645
9.75%	9.7500	9.9877	10.1977	10.2397
10.00%	10.0000	10.2500	10.4713	10.5156
15.00%	15.0000	15.5625	16.0755	16.1798
16.00%	16.0000	16.6400	17.2271	17.3470
17.00%	17.0000	17.7225	18.3892	18.5258
18.00%	18.0000	18.8100	19.5618	19.7164
19.00%	19.0000	19.9025	20.7451	20.9190
20.00%	20.0000	21.0000	21.9393	22.1336

As shown in the chart, if you could receive monthly compounding for the nominal rate of 10.00% you would be ahead by almost 1/2 of 1%. The more frequent the compounding, the higher the effective rate of return. Depending on the length of time and the amount of money invested, this difference could be quite substantial. Conversely, if you are paying a mortgage, the best position is one which compounds annually.

A few examples will help us to identify this important principle.

LONG TERM EFFECT OF VARIOUS DIFFERENCES IN RETURN

$1,000 per year for 35 years

Differences in Return	Differences in Results	% Differences in Results
6% vs. 7%	$111,434 vs. $138,236	24%
6% vs. 8%	$111,434 vs. $177,316	54%
6% vs. 12%	$111,434 vs. $431,663	287%
8% vs. 10%	$172,316 vs. $271,024	57%
8% vs. 12%	$172,316 vs. $431,663	150%
10% vs. 12%	$271,024 vs. $431,663	59%
10% vs. 15%	$271,024 vs. $881,170	225%

Here again, we see the reason prudent investors will shop around for a better return. It pays off!

An early contribution to an investment can have tremendous returns if it is completed at the beginning of the year rather than the end of the year. The following figures provide one example of this fact:

EFFECT OF EARLY CONTRIBUTION FOR 25 YEARS @ 14%

Time of Contribution	Annual Contributions		
	$ 2,000	$ 3,500	$ 5,500
Beginning of Year	$414,665	$725,665	$1,140,330
End of Year	$363,742	$636,548	$1,000,290
Difference	$ 50,923	$ 89,117	$ 140,040

As you readily see, this simple technique will give you a real return that is quite substantial. By moving your Registered Retirement Savings Plan (RRSP) contributions ahead only one year, you earn thousands of dollars more. That is, make your 1988 RRSP contributions in January, 1988 and not wait until later. (Most people would wait until February, 1989 to make their contribution — but a lot more money can be made by doing it early.) Thereafter you continue to contribute each January.

Another interest rate rule which may be helpful is the rule of 72. It can be used to determine the growth rate of investments. By dividing the interest rate into 72, you can calculate the doubling rate for your investment — e.g., 72 ÷ 8 = 9 years.

VALUE OF $1,000 INVESTED

Interest Rate	Doubling Rate*	6 Yrs.	18 Yrs.	30 Yrs.
8%	9 yrs.	1,590	4,000	10,060
10%	7-1/2 yrs.	1,770	5,560	17,450
12%	6 yrs.	1,974	7,690	29,960

* Refers to amount of time before initial investment doubles.

Marginal Tax Rate

How do you decide whether an investment is a good one for you? There are many factors to consider (and they are discussed later in this chapter), but one crucial fact you must know is your marginal tax rate.

First you need to determine your taxable income (line 260, page 2 of your tax return). Locate your federal income tax rate (see chapter two). Then add your provincial income tax rate (see appendix) to the federal rate.

For a taxable income of $22,000 your federal tax rate is 23% + (50% of 23 in Ontario) = 23% + 11.5% = 34.5%. Your tax factor is calculated with this formula:

1.00 ÷ .655 (reciprocal of MTR) = 1.52672

Therefore you must earn $1.53 in before-tax dollars to have $1 of disposable income. In order to purchase a $2,000 item you need to earn $2,000 x 1.53 or $3060!

To determine your MTR for 1988 your calculation is contingent on the proposed tax changes being accepted. The proposed changes appear in chapter two. Keep in mind that the provincial levels of income tax may also change.

Your tax factor is obviously useful for calculating the true cost of items or your investment return.

Real Return

When considering investments make certain that you understand money in terms of before- and after-tax value.

Any return of money that we receive for investment must be viewed as a before-tax return. This concept can best be explained using percentages rather than a number of figures.

Let's suppose that you have an investment bearing 12%, for example. Then your before-tax return is 12%. (For 1987 we'll assume that you have used the tax free $1,000 interest or dividend income credit. In 1988 this credit will be eliminated.) As an Ontario resident your marginal tax rate is approximately 25%. Therefore your after-tax or real return is 12% - 3% (25% of 12) = 9%. However, do remember that the inflation rate is also decreasing this return also.

At this time you may want to stop reading and calculate your real return on your investments. For years Canadians have loaned their monies to the financial institutions as a safe investment. One must question the risk-free investment in these institutions. Who is it a risk for — the lender or borrower? The answer to this question allows us to contemplate the meaning implied when some experts remark that we should buy the banks.

If you are going to borrow a sum of money at the current rate of interest, then the amount you have to repay would be the principal plus the interest (see our earlier discussion on interest rates). This repayment sum is after-tax money because you have already been taxed on it at your marginal tax rate.

A simplified example is the situation of an individual borrowing $1000 at 10% nominal interest. During a one-year period the interest rate would mean the borrower would have to pay back $100 interest plus principal. But remember you must pay the loan back in after-tax dollars. An Ontario resident at the 25% Marginal Tax Rate would have a tax factor of 1.333 (repeating). Therefore this borrower would need to earn $1100 x 1.333 or $1466 in before-tax dollars to pay off the loan. Who borrows such a small amount for such a short period?

Consider this borrowing concept along with the principle of interest costs and you quickly recognize the need to pay off your home mortgage. Unless you can earn more money in other investments (after-tax dollars), generally it is a prudent person who makes every effort to pay off this liability as quickly as possible.

For example, let's suppose you held a $45,000 mortgage at

11% with a 25-year term (renewable in 5 years). If you pay down the principal upon renewal by $5,000, i.e. $42,660-$5,000, you shorten the life of the mortgage 10.33 years and save $74,296 in interest payments! The monthly payment is $683. Even if you can only afford $1,000 extra on the principal, this strategy saves you $27,726.

The following table shows the interest savings you can realize by fast payments of a 13%, $50,000 mortgage:

Monthly Payment	Years to Pay Off	Total Interest Paid
$550	25	$115,000
$575	20	$ 80,800
$600	17	$ 72,400
$625	15	$ 62,500
$655	13	$ 52,180
$705	11	$ 43,060

By spending $155 more on your mortgage every month, you not only save about $72,000 in interest charges (charges you would have to pay with after-tax dollars), but you own the house fourteen years sooner. And remember, these debts are being paid off in after-tax dollars! It is the smart consumer who has a complete mortgage schedule to display the future payments. With this source of data you could see the effects of adjusting payments as suggested. (The Mortgage Insurance Company of Canada offers a free *Mortgage Qualifier* which will help you greatly with these manipulations.)

Business and investment loans are treated more favourably than consumer loans. The interest may be tax deductible at your marginal tax rate. It is wise to check out your possibilities with this rule of thumb. Borrow for tax-deductible business and/or investment purposes, and use your cash for personal needs.

We should make every effort to pay non-deductible debts off first. Debts are a drain on your cash flow. Consumer loans and credit card balances should be paid quickly to avoid payment with expensive after-tax dollars.

You may wish to calculate the real return by this alternative method. A borrower with a Marginal Tax Rate of 40% carries a consumer loan of 15% for his car. The real cost of the loan is calculated as $15 \div 0.60$ (reciprocal of 40% MTR) = 25%. Paying off this loan is like getting an investment return of 25%. By reducing debt, you are removing a psychological barrier against the ability to invest.

Retirement Income

Now it seems appropriate to determine the amount of money that you will need to maintain your accepted lifestyle. The three principal sources of this income are from your "guaranteed" government pensions, your company pension, and your private investments. First we must calculate how much money you need today for living expenses. Then consult the inflation/interest table in the appendix. For example if your annual requirement is $30,000, your calculation is as follows:

$30,000 x 3.21 (6% inflation rate over 20 years) = $96,300

Hopefully you will receive pension money from Old Age Security and the Canada Pension Plan. The following chart is helpful in determining this amount:

PROJECTED GOVERNMENT PENSIONS

YEAR	OAS	CPP*	TOTAL
1990	$ 4,004	$ 6,824	$10,828
1995	$ 4,871	$ 8,303	$13,174
2000	$ 5,926	$10,101	$16,028
2005	$ 7,210	$12,290	$19,500
2010	$ 8,773	$14,953	$23,725
2015	$10,673	$18,192	$28,865
2020	$12,986	$22,133	$35,119

* Maximum CPP
* Based on 4% indexing factor

The best advice is to check with your personnel people to determine your approximate company pension. (Once again the inflation chart may be used to project a specific indexing.)

By subtracting your combined government and company pensions from your future annual needs, you will have calculated how much private investment money must be generated. Now you have the minimum sum of money which will be required for your lifestyle needs.

For a more detailed discussion of pensions, how they work and what you can expect from them, consider *Looking After The Future* (1987). It was written by two contributing editors to the *Canadian MoneySaver* and is available from our office.

INVESTMENT CONCEPTS

Considerations of Investment Decisions

You are aware of the importance your marginal tax rate has on your investment decisions. There are still other factors which you should consider when going through these decision-making processes. Canada Savings Bonds will be used as a specific reference for this example.

The first consideration is the safety factor. How solid is the investment? What are my chances of keeping my principal investment? Canada Savings Bonds (CSBs) are guaranteed by the government. The safety factor is high. But you may question your safety once the inflation and tax costs are deducted from the yield.

Liquidity refers to how quickly you can get your money returned to you if it is necessary. Is there any penalty for liquidating early? What amount of money will you receive and how soon? CSBs (1986) could be liquidated with interest after February 1, 1987.

Your rate of return or yield provides value to you for making this investment. What do you receive from this transaction? The rate of return on CSBs is announced a few weeks before the sale of this investment vehicle.

The term can vary considerably on many investments. This time period should be considered with respect to current and future trends. You may wish to deposit your money in CSBs for the maximum term of seven years, unless you might want to liquidate earlier.

Obviously you need to understand the tax implications of this investment vehicle. Is the yield treated as interest, dividends or capital gains? In the case of CSBs you expect interest treatment. These tax costs will be discussed in chapter two.

Does the investment have inflation protection? Some investments such as real estate and gold have withstood the ravages of inflation in the past. As discussed earlier, when you're contemplating buying an interest-bearing product such as CSBs, you should discount the inflation rate to calculate the real return.

The management effort necessary to maintain or monitor this investment should be kept in mind. In other words, how easy or time consuming is it to manage? Do you have ongoing cash flow to reinvest? Are there specific times when the investment should be liquidated? Do you handle these decisions? Are they automatic?

The foregoing factors tend to be the major questions to have answered before the investment is purchased. As you research or become more knowledgeable about specific investments, you will acquire the expertise to include additional questions which are pertinent to the chosen investment.

Risk and Reward

Conventional wisdom suggests that in order to attain a high rate of return (reward) on an investment, you must accept the high risk of loss. Loss usually means the possibility of at least a partial loss of your invested capital. This relationship also implies that you have the potential for a greater reward when you accept a greater risk.

The accompanying graph illustrates this concept.

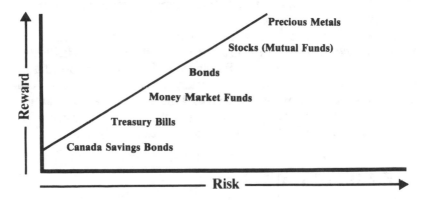

Purchasing Canada Savings Bonds, for example, would be low on the risk and reward side of the graph. This graph indicates that the best reward possible at almost no risk would be obtained from CSBs, Treasury Bills and Money Market Funds, which are low and left on the graph line.

Once we move away from these interest-bearing instruments we must accept a greater degree of risk. You would be moving up the risk/reward line with the following investments: bonds, mortgages, stocks (mutual funds) and precious metals.

Be wary when you are offered a superb opportunity for profit with little risk. High profit and high risk tend to go hand-in-hand. Evaluate these investments with the risk factor in mind.

However, if you accept a high-risk investment you should anticipate a high return such as 50-100% over five years. Whatever investment you select, do so with the feeling that you can comfortably live with it in your portfolio. Your sleep factor, that is, how well you sleep at night, will or should help you decide on the best investment for you.

Since you have budgeted for savings, it may be helpful to divide your investment fund into categories according to risk. (This decision is made once necessities and fixed expenses have been accounted for in your strategic plan.) Each category such as low, medium and high risk could be allocated a specific percentage of your investment funds.

There are four major types of investments: cash, fixed-income, equity and tangible assets. Cash instruments include Treasury Bills, short-term deposits, and Canada Savings Bonds. The longer-term, fixed-income investments include preferred shares and quality bonds. The most common type of equity is stocks (mutual funds). Tangible assets consist of collectibles, real estate and precious metals. Each type is accompanied by its own level of risk/reward.

It is also important to note that various investments can be affected by economic conditions. For example, when the inflation rate is low and interest rates decrease (as in 1981-82), bond and stocks soared. When an inflationary period begins, tangible assets will become more attractive. Due to factors such as interest rate, market risk and leveraging, it is a wise investor who does not place all his eggs in one basket and hedges his bet.

THE PRIORITY APPROACH

Earlier in this chapter we demonstrated the need to use our money in a strategic manner rather than purchase whatever is the latest fad or in a random fashion. The priority approach is a conceptual approach to money management and this financial planning process is generally logical and practical for most of us. It is designed to help us focus on the various stages of investments and how to proceed through these stages.

The priority pyramid or investment pyramid illustrates very safe investments as the basic foundation and first stage before future involvement. Here we find bank accounts and insurance. As we proceed along the stages towards the top, we encounter very risky and speculative investments such as commodities, art and futures options.

The following priority pyramid will help you visually focus on the step-by-step process of this technique:.

PRIORITY/INVESTMENT PYRAMID

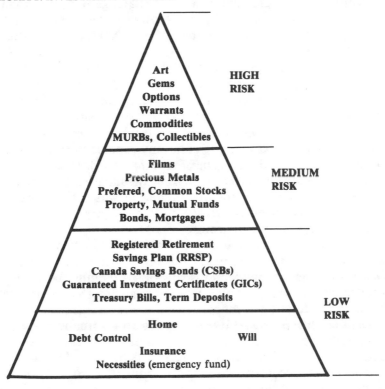

Stage One

The first stage in this process deals with expenditures which are relatively fixed. The family has a commitment to a fairly regular payment schedule for these necessities. At this stage your budget will be planned to handle these ongoing expenses.

The first use of your savings may be to set up an emergency fund. Shop around to get the best return on this liquid fund. This money is set aside for a financial crisis which we hope never comes. It is not money to pay off the credit cards or purchase a want (e.g., a new car). If you decide to place this money in a bank account, keep it separate from your other bank accounts. (Different bank accounts for different purposes tends to be a good idea for your savings programme.)

This fund provides you with peace of mind in case of sickness or job loss, for example. Most experts suggest the pool of money should be equivalent to three-to-six months' salary. Another possibility is to stash up to 10 per cent of your investment portfolio in liquid investments. Investments may include a daily-interest savings account, Canada Savings Bonds, Treasury Bills and Money Market Funds. However, be aware that the proposed tax reform will eliminate the $1,000 interest/dividend deduction for 1988.

A protection plan is purchased through the various types of insurance which you require. The order of purchase may be disability, home, car and life, depending upon your personal circumstances. Independent brokers who can shop the market for you are an excellent source of quotes. However, do compare more than prices with single-company representatives also. A newly released book, *Shoppers' Guide to Canadian Life Insurance Policies and Prices*, provides detailed explanations for mortgage, group and life insurance. It was written by Bill McLeod, a contributor to *Canadian MoneySaver*, and is available through our office.

Your estate plan should also be established at this time. You will need to decide how much money to leave and to whom. Obviously, the tax implications of doing this must be carefully considered. Your will is the package plan for this manoeuvre. For further details see chapter eight.

Debt control is crucial if you wish to attain financial success. Non-deductible debts should be eliminated in favour of tax-deductible loans. But the best kind of debt is no debt at all!

You could predetermine what amount of debt you will encounter based on your previous financial plans. If possible this debt load should be limited to major items. By comparing interest rates through a few financial institutions, you will obtain the best rate. At each institution ask about a specific amount of money, the interest rate, and the total monthly repayment cost. This planned borrowing should save you money.

One form of debt, the credit card, is abused by thousands of Canadians. It is so easy to use the card when you don't have the money on hand. Often the spending is for things you don't need. Every time you use your card(s) you are using someone else's money. And, there is a price to pay for this service. The borrowing cost is exorbitant. Avoid these costs if you can.

So you can use cash to avoid possible abuse of your card(s) and probably limit your spending. Or, if you pay your account in full each month, you are using solid financial techniques. Almost all cards have an interest-free payment period — if you pay the account in full by the due date. This "float" ranges from 15-60 days, depending on the time of purchase. Some cards, like Bank of Montreal's MasterCard, charge no user fees. The principal residence continues to be a tax shelter — tax free — in Canada. Therefore, it is generally the first and best investment for most of us. Paying off your mortgage as quickly as possible will permit you to invest in other instruments sooner.

Stage Two

The second defensive phase is also considered low risk. Once our income and assets are protected, we will begin to examine our retirement needs. Investments at this level are relatively safe. Each individual should strive for the best return by shopping around.

It also becomes increasingly important to consider the tax implications of your investment decisions and what tax incentives are available. But an investment must still be a sound investment without the tax considerations.

As your money increases, funds can be shifted into instruments which will permit you to receive a better return — for example, from Canada Savings Bonds to Treasury Bills. At this stage most investments are relatively liquid. In order to defer taxes, RRSPs are purchased. The guaranteed plans are available through various financial institutions. An examination of mutual funds which may be placed inside an RRSP follows in chapter five.

Stages Three and Four

Once this solid base has been set up, you may wish to start investing in riskier vehicles for growth possibilities. These final two stages are more aggressive. Personal education of each investment option should be undertaken before these investments are contemplated and placed in your portfolio. Here we are looking for a hedge against inflation.

Thousands of Canadians are diluting their risk by investing in mutual funds (the fastest-growing investment). This pooling of funds with others should minimize risk. Some other advantages include the low initial investment required, portfolio diversification through the funds, and professional management. In spite of these advantages, the investor should study all aspects before selecting a fund. The mutual fund chapter (five) will help you.

The final stage deals with the most speculative and risky "opportunities". You have the possibility of high growth, but with the real risk of loss. You need a great deal of personal expertise to purchase commodities, warrants, and collectibles. Since these are not safe investments, you will not find information here on them. One must question whether speculation is an investment form or not.

Your family's position in this priority approach will be affected by your age, income, expenses, number of dependents, savings and other changing conditions. Your personal comfort level has a significant bearing on your development too.

To diminish the degree of risk, remember to diversify — do not put all your eggs in one basket.

INVESTMENT USES

You are often faced with the dilemma of deciding whether you should own or loan money. For example, you may loan your funds to the bank to earn interest in one of various forms such as a deposit account, short-term/long-term deposit or mortgage account. Each investment form will bring with it a different interest return.

On the other hand you may wish to be an owner and buy the bank. By purchasing the bank stock you share in the profits of the institution. The value of this investment increases when the bank prospers and its stock becomes more attractive. Your stock earnings and/or dividends may vary depending on the growth possibilities.

An investor may look for growth or income options. Debt investments, such as mortgages, yield a fixed income. Equity investment may pay you with dividends, appreciation, or both.

"Blue-chip" stocks are those which have provided steady profit for years. If an investor wants to be more aggressive, new or younger companies offer the possibilities of greater capital gains (or losses). These agressive growth stocks are for investors who can afford to lose money. Whatever type is selected, generally you invest in stocks for long-term appreciation. Depending on your age, you will need to adjust the percentage of your investment portfolio which contains growth stocks.

The income investments, such as bonds, will generate income now. As you grow older and move closer to retirement, it is wise to shift out of growth and into more income investments. Remember, mutual funds (and family of funds) will also permit you to follow this strategy quite easily.

With the priority pyramid we examined the low vs. the high risk options available to you. Generally the rule is that the greater the opportunity for investment gain, the greater the risk of loss. Even on a "safe" investment like a term deposit there may be some degree of risk. The highest return offered could be "guaranteed" by a relatively small regional trust company. Consumer beware and be wary.

Investors should be aware of the tax advantages or disadvantages of various investments. There are usually good reasons for tax incentives being offered. Do not be attracted to an investment only because there is some tax advantage. Some investment earnings are treated differently. The smart investor knows how interest, dividend and capital gains are taxed (see chapter two).

Are your investments going to require personal or professional management? You know your personal capabilities. Not all professional managers are equal. You would be wise to learn as much as possible about the manager or management group before making your investment decision. Interview several brokers to discover the investment advice you can expect and whether or not your personalities are compatible. Perhaps a discount broker will serve you better than a full-service broker.

SUMMARY

This chapter has outlined the major considerations which should be implemented and practiced before becoming an active investor. With this background in place and your elementary education complete, you will move into the secondary and upper levels of your investment acumen. The following chapters will assist you and steer you through this sometimes confusing maze.

REFERENCES

Looking After the Future (1987) by Patrick Longhurst and Rose Marie Earle $12.95 (paper), 224 pages.

Canadian MoneySaver (nine times annually) by a national team of financial experts $24.75, no advertising. Write: Box 370, Bath, Ontario K0H 1G0, (613) 352-7448. Free copy on request.

The Information Centre, Canadian Life and Health Insurance Association, 20 Queen Street West, Suite 2500, Toronto, Ontario M5H 352.

Mortgage Insurance Company of Canada, Box 12, 1 Dundas Street West, Suite 1600, Toronto, Ontario M5G 1Z3 (416) 977-6254. Regional offices throughout Canada.

Shoppers' Guide to Canadian Life Insurance Polices and Prices (1987) by Bill McLeod $9.95 (paper), 267 pages.

CHAPTER 2

TAXATION AND INVESTMENTS

By Don Zinyk

INTRODUCTION

"A penny saved is a penny earned" according to Benjamin Franklin. Though the complicated world of investments and taxation was something well beyond even his foresight, his often-quoted adage still holds true with an update: reducing the taxes on your investments increases your effective rate of return.

The purpose of this chapter is not to tell you what to invest in — that's the job of an investment counsellor — but rather to give you some tax-planning ideas for saving money on the investments you already own or may be considering. It should also be noted that these are only the basics of investment tax saving. Detailed tax planning depends totally on your individual personal tax situation, and is best handled by your own professional advisor who is aware of that situation and can help you fully assess the benefits and risks involved with it.

While the opportunities to make the most significant tax savings are quite often attached to the most sophisticated investments, there are also opportunities to save tax dollars on investments as basic as Canada Savings Bonds and guaranteed investment certificates.

FIGURING OUT YOUR INCOME TAX BRACKET

Before the current alternatives for saving or minimizing income taxes on investments are discussed, it is important to explain how an individual's overall tax rate has been affected by the recent White Paper on Tax Reform presented to Canadians on June 18, 1987 by Finance Minister Michael Wilson.

For 1987, individuals will find themselves in one of 10 existing federal tax brackets which are as follows:

1987 TAX RATES

Taxable Income	Federal Marginal Rates	Combined Federal/Provincial Marginal Rates*
0 to $ 1,318	6%	9.0%
$ 1,319-$ 2,638	16%	24.0%
$ 2,639-$ 5,278	17%	25.5%
$ 5,279-$ 7,917	18%	27.0%
$ 7,918-$13,196	19%	28.5%
$13,197-$18,475	20%	30.0%
$18,476-$23,754	23%	34.5%
$23,755-$36,591	25%	37.5%
$36,592-$63,346	30%	45.0%
$63,347 & over	34%	51.0%

* Assuming a 50% provincial tax rate, ignoring federal or provincial surtaxes.

However, for 1988 and subsequent years, the White Paper proposes to condense the number of tax brackets to three as follows:

1988 TAX RATES

Taxable Income	Federal Marginal Rate	Combined Federal/Provincial Marginal Rate*
0-$27,500	17%	25.5%
$27,501-$55,000	26%	39.0%
$55,001 & over	29%	43.5%

* Assumes a 50% provincial rate, ignoring federal and provincial surtaxes.

Before one gets too excited over the reduction in the federal tax rates and number of brackets, it is important to recognize that the tax base on which the lower rates will be applied will also be broadened. Personal exemptions, such as the basic and married exemptions, pension income deduction, age deduction, tuition fees deduction, education deduction, charitable donations, etc. will be converted to tax credits instead of being deductions in computing taxable income. If all other factors remain the same, individuals will find that their 1988 taxable income will increase by about $5,500 to $10,000 in a typical situation over the comparable 1987 amount as a result of the conversion of these deductions to tax credits. This may push the individual into a higher than anticipated tax bracket for 1988.

INVESTMENT INCOME DEDUCTION

One of the easiest ways to ensure that you are saving as many tax dollars as you can on your investments is to make maximum use of the investment income deduction available to all individuals. Unfortunately, the deduction will only be available until the end of 1987, since the June 18, 1987 White Paper proposes to eliminate this deduction.

Thus, in 1987 you may deduct up to $1,000 of the total Canadian interest income and grossed-up dividends net of certain interest expense in computing your taxable income. The amount eligible for this deduction is reduced by any interest expense you have incurred on money borrowed to earn the eligible interest and/or dividends. (Interest expense incurred on funds borrowed to contribute to an RRSP before November 13, 1981, to acquire foreign investments, to operate a business, to invest in a partnership, or to acquire shares in a non-arm's length corporation does not reduce the amount eligible.) Some opportunities to maximize the income you have available for this deduction for 1987 are:

Monitor Corporation Investments. Investment income received from a non-arm's length corporation does not qualify for the deduction. Accordingly, if you invest funds through a corporation, you should retain sufficient funds outside the corporation to generate at least $1,000 of eligible income.

Spousal Transfers. If you are not able to fully use your investment income deduction because of insufficient taxable income, you may be able to transfer the unused portion to your spouse. Like the pension income deduction, the investment income deduction is transferable only to the extent that your claim for the married exemption is reduced by your spouse's income.

For Seniors. If you are 65 or over, you might elect to treat the income portion of unregistered annuities (i.e., annuities other than those from an RRSP, income-averaging annuity contract or a deferred profit sharing plan), as interest. Because this income amount would otherwise be treated as pension income, the election is useful if you have already fully used the $1,000 pension income deduction for 1987 (because of other income qualifying for that deduction) but not the $1,000 investment income deduction. You may make this election for one year without being bound to it in future years.

Borrow For Foreign Investments. As noted previously, the investment income deduction is only reduced by interest expense incurred on borrowings to purchase Canadian debt and equity investments. Interest on funds borrowed to generate foreign interest and dividend income does not reduce this deduction. For this reason it may be advantageous to borrow to purchase foreign securities while using available funds to purchase Canadian securities. If you do this, you should ensure that you are able to trace the interest expense to purchases of foreign securities.

If you have fully utilized your $1,000 investment income deduction in 1987, you might consider deferring interest and other investment income until 1988 if you will benefit from lower tax rates. This can be accomplished fairly easily in the case of short-term investments, where you should consider reinvesting term deposits and the like coming due between now and the end of 1987 at new terms maturing, say, early in 1988 rather than late 1987.

INTEREST INCOME AND THE THREE-YEAR ACCRUAL RULE

With investment contracts such as mortgages, Canada Savings Bonds and other debt obligations such as guaranteed investment certificates, you can save money by choosing the most appropriate method for reporting interest income.

Since 1982, taxpayers have been required to report compounding interest income at least every three years (the three-year rule) unless they elect to accrue the interest income annually. When interest income has been reported annually on a particular investment, this method must be continued for that investment until it matures. Under the three-year rule, the accrued interest which must be reported is only that portion accruing from January 1, 1982. Interest accruing up to that date will generally not be taxed until received or receivable.

(Also, certain investment contracts purchased before November 13, 1981 are not subject to these rules or, if not excluded altogether, are subject to a transitional rule such that the first "three-year" accrual date will be deemed to occur in 1988. At that time, the interest accrued from 1982 to 1988 will be subject to tax. Investment contracts purchased after November 12, 1981 will be subject to the three-year accrual rules starting on the first day of the third calendar year after the contract was purchased, and every third year thereafter.)

If you own these types of interest-bearing securities, you might consider electing to declare the interest earned annually, rather than using the cash method or the three-year rule, to avoid the disadvantage of having large amounts of interest income being included in income in one year. This can result in the interest income being taxed at higher marginal rates in the year it is received or declared, but remember that in 1988 your tax rate may be lower than in 1987.

It may also be beneficial if you have not fully utilized your $1,000 investment income deduction in 1987. (Be aware, however, that you may end up prepaying tax in years after 1987.)

It is important to note that you do not have to use the same basis of reporting for all interest income. Rather, the interest income on one type of contract may be reported on one basis, while the interest on another contract may be reported on another basis. You must, however, be consistent in the treatment of each investment contract from year to year.

Similar rules apply to annuities and life insurance policies.

THE DIVIDEND VERSUS INTEREST DEBATE

A common question facing the investor is whether to purchase investments which pay interest or dividends. Before we give away the secret to knowing which is better, an examination of the rules concerning the taxation of dividends is in order.

Dividends — whether they be cash or stock — must be declared on a cash basis (i.e., in the year in which they are received). When you receive a taxable dividend from a taxable Canadian corporation, you must include in your income an amount equal (for 1987) to 1.33 times the actual dividend received. You may then claim a credit against your federal tax equal to 16-2/3% of the "grossed-up" dividend. (This "dividend tax credit" exists because dividends are paid out of corporate earnings on which the corporation has already paid tax). The June 18, 1987 White Paper proposes that for 1988 and subsequent taxation years an individual will have to include in income an amount equal to 1.25 times the actual dividend received and be entitled to a federal dividend tax credit equal to 13-1/3% of the grossed-up dividend.

What is the significance of this for you, the investor? One of the basics that you must take into account when you choose any investment is its after-tax rate of return; that rate is quite different for investments paying the same stated rate in interest and dividends. Chart I provides a dividend/interest yield comparison for 1987, based on a provincial tax rate of 50%.

CHART I
1987
Dividend/Interest Yield Comparison

Dividend Yield	Equivalent Interest Yield for Following Taxable Income Brackets		
	$23,755 36,951	$36,952 63,346	$63,347 and over
4%	5.38%	5.38%	5.39%
6%	8.06%	8.08%	8.08%
8%	10.75%	10.77%	10.78%
10%	13.44%	13.46%	13.47%
12%	16.13%	16.15%	16.17%
14%	18.82%	18.84%	18.86%

For example, if your earnings are in the tax bracket of $23,755 to $36,951, and you have the choice between an investment yielding 4% in dividends or 5% in interest, the dividend is your better choice — you need to earn an interest rate of at least 5.38% to be equal.

A good rule of thumb for 1987 is that to obtain an equivalent interest rate, multiply the dividend yield by 1.35. Put another way, $4 of interest will yield the same amount after tax as a $3 dividend.

Chart II provides the same comparison for 1988, based on the federal tax rates proposed in the June 18, 1987 White Paper, and on a provincial tax rate of 50%.

CHART II
1988
Dividend/Interest Yield Comparison

Dividend Yield	Equivalent Interest Yield for Following Taxable Income Brackets		
	$ 0 27,500	$27,501 55,000	$55,001 and over
4%	5.03%	5.03%	5.04%
6%	7.54%	7.55%	7.55%
8%	10.05%	10.07%	10.07%
10%	12.57%	12.58%	12.59%
12%	15.08%	15.10%	15.11%
14%	17.59%	17.62%	17.62%

A good rule of thumb for 1988 and beyond is that to obtain an equivalent interest rate, multiply the dividend yield by 1.26. In other words, $5 of interest will yield the same amount after tax as a $4 dividend.

Some investments give rise to a capital gain. Again, different types of investments attract different rates of taxation, and it is the after-tax rate of return you should use as a guide. Chart III provides an overview of the various rates of tax in effect for three different types of investments in 1987, based on a provincial rate of taxation of 50%, and listed for income earners in three tax brackets. It shows you the comparative rates of tax you would pay on each dollar of income not eligible for the $1,000 investment deduction earned as interest, dividends or capital gains. A similar overview is provided in Chart IV for 1988.

CHART III
1987 Marginal Rate of Taxation

Taxable Income	Interest	Dividend	Capital Gain
$23,755-$36,951	38.25%	17.00%	19.12%
$36,952-$63,346	45.90%	27.18%	22.95%
$63,347 & over	52.02%	35.35%	26.01%

Rates give effect to the federal surtax for 1987. Rates do not give effect to the $1,000 interest and dividend deduction, the capital gains exemption or the alternative minimum tax. With reference to dividend income, marginal rates are based on the actual amount received, not the grossed-up amount.

CHART IV
1988 Marginal Rate of Taxation

Taxable Income	Interest	Dividend	Capital Gain
$ 0-$27,500	26.01%	7.01%	17.34%
$27,501-$55,000	39.78%	24.22%	26.52%
$55,000 & over	44.37%	29.96%	29.58%

Rates give effect to the federal surtax for 1988. Rates do not give effect to the capital gains exemption or the alternative minimum tax. With reference to dividend income, marginal rates are based on the actual amount received, not the grossed-up amount.

MORE ABOUT CAPITAL GAINS

Currently, if you dispose of a capital property, one-half of the capital gain realized on the disposition must be included in your income. The June 18, 1987 White Paper proposes to increase the proportion of capital gains that will be subject to tax commencing in 1988. Starting in 1988 two-thirds of capital gains will be included in your income with a further increase to three-quarters of capital gains in 1990. Even with the proposed lower rates of 1988 and subsequent years, the effect of this increase in the portion of capital gains subject to tax will increase the tax burden on capital gains.

Since 1985, individuals who are resident in Canada throughout a taxation year have been eligible for a lifetime exemption for capital gains. The present limit of $100,000 was slated to gradually increase to the maximum lifetime limit of $500,000 (taxable capital gains of $250,000) by 1990. The June 18, 1987 White Paper proposes to cap the exemption at the present $100,000 level for 1988 and subsequent years, subject to an exception for dispositions of qualified farm property and shares of a small business corporation.

The capital gains exemption takes the form of a deduction from income in computing taxable income. It is important to remember that it is a discretionary deduction — there are circumstances in which it may not be beneficial to claim the exemption in a year. For instance, you may forgo a claim in a low-income year if you anticipate large gains in a subsequent year which would be taxed at a substantially higher marginal tax rate. In addition, if you sold property which has been subject to tax in a foreign country, you may choose not to claim the exemption to the extent that the foreign tax can be applied against your Canadian tax liability. (You should note that a capital gain realized on the disposition of a principal residence remains tax-free and does not affect the calculation of an individual's capital gain exemption.)

Farmers are not subject to the phase-in rules on the sale of qualified farm property. An exemption of $250,000, less any exemption claimed on the disposition of any other capital property in the year or preceding years, may be claimed for 1985 and subsequent years. Furthermore, farmers may claim a capital gains reserve (over a maximum 10-year period) in connection with the sale of qualified farm property and claim a capital gains exemption as the proceeds are received (and the capital gain included in income) in future years.

The June 18, 1987 White Paper proposes to allow individuals an exemption of $500,000 for capital gains realized on the disposition of shares of a small business corporation commencing in 1988. However, to the extent an individual has fully utilized the $500,000 exemption on the disposition of either qualified farm property or shares of a small business corporation, a further exemption of $100,000 on other property will not be permitted. The June 18, 1987 White Paper also contained a further change to the capital gains exemption which may affect your ability to claim the exemption commencing in 1988. It is proposed that after 1987 your net taxable capital gains eligible for the exemption be reduced by your cumulative investment losses deducted in 1988 and subsequent years. Basically, an investment loss will occur where your investment expenses (including tax shelter write-offs) exceed your investment income. These rules may severely impair the ability of investors with large carrying costs on their investment portfolio from claiming the capital gains exemption.

Finally, it is important to note that Revenue Canada, in order to monitor compliance with the capital gains exemption, now requires individuals to file a tax return (even if no tax is payable) for any year in which they have a taxable capital gain or have disposed of property. Failure to do so may result in a denial of the exemption for that year.

USING THE CAPITAL GAINS EXEMPTION
FOR FUN AND PROFIT

The capital gains exemption provides many people with an excellent opportunity to realize tax-free capital gains. In many cases, due to the changes proposed to the exemption pronounced in the June 18, 1987 White Paper, consideration should be given to accelerating the recognition of capital gains to 1987, especially if you anticipate that you will have portfolio carrying charges and tax shelter write-offs in future years in excess of your investment income.

It is important, however, to remember also that depending on your personal tax position, capital gains which are otherwise tax-free may be subject to alternative minimum tax. If you plan to claim a sizeable capital gain exemption, you should seek professional advice to determine if minimum tax will apply in your situation.

Some of the ways in which you may be able to utilize the capital gains exemption to your advantage include:

Personal Acquisitions Of Assets. Generally, the capital gains exemption creates a bias towards holding appreciating assets personally as opposed to through a registered retirement savings plan or a corporation. The reason for this is that the capital gains exemption is only available to individuals. Therefore, you should seek out and hold personally, investments which will generate capital gains.

Sale Of Marketable Securities To An RRSP. You can transfer investments which qualify for an RRSP to a self-administered RRSP either by way of a direct sale or as a contribution. On transfer the investment is considered to have been disposed of at its fair market value. As a result, a capital gain may be realized which would qualify for the capital gains exemption. However, any capital loss realized on such a transfer is deemed to be nil. The transfer of an investment in the form of a contribution may be an attractive alternative if you don't have enough cash to make the contribution at the particular time. The sale of investments to a self-administered RRSP provides an opportunity to remove cash from an RRSP and use the funds to pay off loans where the interest is not tax deductible or to purchase personal-use assets.

This idea, notwithstanding, you must remember that dividend tax credits earned on dividends received by an RRSP do not flow out to the owner of the RRSP and the entire capital gain realized by an RRSP is taxed when you withdraw the funds from the RRSP. Consequently, the capital appreciation in the RRSP must outweigh these adverse factors in order to make this a sound investment decision.

Shareholders' Agreements And Wills. The capital gains exemption has changed the entire tax game as far as shareholders' agreements and wills are concerned. You and your professional advisor should perform a review of your will and shareholders' agreements to determine what changes are necessary to take maximum advantage of the capital gains exemption.

OTHER IDEAS — TRANSFER OF DIVIDENDS ELECTION

If you are married, the personal exemption which you can claim for your spouse is reduced by his or her income in excess of a base amount ($520 for 1987). If the spouse receives dividends from Canadian corporations, it is the grossed-up amount (i.e., 1.33% of the actual dividend for 1987) that is included in income.

If you claim a personal exemption for your spouse, you may elect to include in your income the dividends he or she receives from Canadian corporations. This election can only be made if the amount of the personal exemption you claim in respect of your spouse will be increased. Also remember that, if you make this election, all of your spouse's Canadian dividend income must be included in your tax return.

This option is contrary to the usual objective of income splitting — if made, the income will be transferred from the lower income spouse to the higher one. The advantage arises because the dividend tax credit then becomes available to the spouse reporting the dividend income. There can, however, be situations where this election is not beneficial. For 1987, you must look carefully at the amount of dividend income, your tax rate, how much of your spouse's investment income deduction can be transferred to you, and whether or not you have fully used your investment income deduction. This really means you will have to calculate your tax liability both with and without your spouse's dividends included in your income in order to determine the best result.

TAX SHELTERS

Most tax shelter investments, by their nature, tend to carry a significant degree of risk. Unfortunately, the related income tax deductions sometimes cause investors to downplay or even ignore normal business and investment considerations. Even after taking into account the tax benefits, the end result of a tax shelter frequently can be an actual cash loss.

While a full discussion of various shelters and their tax treatments are well beyond the scope of this chapter, let three guidelines remain:

- Tax shelters are only for the most sophisticated of investors, and for the most part should not be entered into without professional advice.
- The government is tightening the rules concerning tax shelters, and what appears as a bright prospect today may not always be so.
- The prime consideration for any proposed tax shelter investment should be whether it has a reasonable expectation of profit, exclusive of its tax shelter characteristics. Once that has been established, you can then go on to consider the extent to which the tax shelter feature increases its attractiveness.

A FINAL WORD ABOUT INVESTMENTS

While the after-tax rate of return is definitely a consideration in choosing an investment, there are significant others — security, liquidity and inflation — that you also need to look at. Your personal goals and your degree of financial sophistication in the investment that's best for you, and there are two pieces of down-home advice that always apply:

Know Something About What You're Investing In. If you were going to spend $5,000 on a second-hand car, you'd probably kick more than a few tires before you handed over your cash. You should use the same scrutiny and conduct the same research before you tie up your money in any investment. That includes finding out about the tax-planning strategies you can use to get the most out of the investment.

If It Doesn't Feel Good, Don't Do It. Rely on your intuition. If you're not comfortable with a proposed investment — for whatever reason — then look elsewhere. Sure, rags-to-riches stories encourage us to be risk-takers, but few of us can afford to take the many losses that often precede the big win. Also, unless you're completely comfortable with your investment, you may not recognize when to make the move that will enable you to hit the jackpot.

CHAPTER 3

THE STRATEGY FOR INVESTING

By Chuck Chakrapani

GETTING RICH SLOWLY

Basic Principles

Most of us feel that there are magical ways of increasing our wealth, if only we knew them. We have all heard stories of stock market wizards who have translated $1,000 into one million dollars in six months. We wish we knew their tricks.

It is true that some people have done stunningly well with their investments. But then many people have done well in lotteries and gambling as well.

The fact is that only a very few investors really make big money. There is no sure way to get rich quick. But there are sure ways to get rich slowly.

Four Ingredients of Wealth

If you want to be certain of getting rich, you need four ingredients: Time, Discipline, Knowledge and Strategy.

Time. If you invest $20,000 at 12% interest, you will have $35,240 at the end of five years. But if you continue to leave it for another 30 years, you will have well over one million dollars. Often called the "magic of compounding", this example shows how your money grows faster the longer you are willing to wait.

Discipline. Lack of discipline arises out of two factors: greed and impatience. They are related. When we hear someone tell us how easy it is to make money, we get tempted. Greed takes over. Although we know that there is really no sure-fire way to get rich quick, we take the chance. Our impatience with our slow-but-sure program becomes our undoing. Therefore, the second factor to remember is discipline. If others are getting richer faster, let them.

Knowledge. To make money we should know how the world works, what will make your money work hard for you, why certain events take place, and how your money is affected by such events.

Strategy. It is not enough to be willing to wait and it is not enough to be disciplined, and it is not even enough if you know a lot about how the world works. You should also know how to build wealth the quickest possible way without taking chances with your money. You should know how to use your knowledge effectively. This is where strategy comes in. When luck does not play a part, a person with a strategy will achieve his or her goal faster than the one who is just hoping to get rich. Having a strategy is like having a road map and a compass when you go treasure hunting.

Four Ingredients of Wealth

1. Time
2. Discipline
3. Knowledge
4. Strategy

A Strategy for Getting Rich Slowly ... Fast

Of the four ingredients, the first two — Time and Discipline — can be provided only by you. Here we will talk about Knowledge and Strategy.

In this context, knowledge simply means understanding how the economy works, what makes the value of investments go up and down. Based on our understanding of the world, we will also develop a strategy for investing.

It is important to note that it is not crucial for you to agree with everything that is said here. But it is important to have some organized view of the world to invest intelligently. Moreover, an investment strategy should be personal. No matter what I say, if you are not comfortable with it, modify it until you are comfortable. Once you decide on a strategy, stick with it.

How the World Works: A Crash Course in Economics

The explanation provided here is highly oversimplified. Economic conditions are affected by monetary and fiscal policies, global events, unforeseen social and technological breakthroughs and political realities. The purpose of this section is simply to present one view of how economic conditions may change, thereby affecting your investments.

Sometimes the stock market goes up and other times down. Sometimes interest rates are high, sometimes they are low. Sometimes inflation is high, sometimes it is low. Sometimes unemployment is high, sometimes it is low. All of this affects your investments. Therefore we may want to understand why these things happen.

In the sections that follow, I present an oversimplified view of how these things happen. The idea is not to turn you into an economist, but simply to enable you to quickly see the interrelationships among different economic conditions and how they affect the value of our investments.

How good times can lead to bad times. Let us start somewhere in time. Everyone is relatively prosperous. Consumers find that they earn enough and house prices are affordable. They start buying.

The demand for houses goes up. But there are only so many houses on the market. Therefore the prices of houses go up. When house prices go up, it becomes profitable for builders to build more houses. So they start building houses. But this takes time. Meanwhile, the prices of houses go up even further. The house prices go up to such an extent that people cannot afford them anymore. Now fewer and fewer people want to buy houses. Because there is less demand, house prices fall. The new houses which were started at the boom are now ready for sale. Although there are even more houses, there are few buyers. The house prices fall further.

Because there is no demand for houses, builders don't build houses. The workers don't have work. Unemployment increases. Unemployed people have less money than the employed, and the unemployed buy fewer goods and services. Because they buy less, the demand for goods and services falls. Industries manufacture less goods. Because they manufacture less, they need fewer employees. So more employees lose their jobs. Demand goes down even further. Unemployment increases even more. And so on.

How are your investments affected? With so much

unemployment around, who can afford to buy all the luxury goods manufactured by different companies? The industries cannot sell what they make and realize a profit. Their stock prices decrease in value. Because stock prices fall in value nobody wants to invest in the stock market. The demand for stocks falls. It becomes difficult to make money in the stock market.

How bad times can lead to fast times. All this creates a problem for the government. Politicians cannot get re-elected when industries don't do well, when unemployment is high and investors are not interested in investing in industries. So the government starts to create jobs.

It does so by giving incentives to industries to produce more. The government itself spends more, which creates more jobs. The government may also lower interest rates, which makes it easy for consumers to borrow and spend on items like refrigerators, cars and the like. Because consumers spend more, industries start producing more. Because industries produce more, they employ more people. Unemployment falls. People have more money. They buy more. And so on.

At the same time, because most people have jobs and they can easily borrow, the demand for many goods and services increases. Because the demand is high, the prices of goods and services go up. Because prices have gone up, workers demand more money. When their wages are increased, they have even more money to buy. The demand grows. The price increases. So it goes. Wages rise to catch up with prices and prices increase because there is so much money around. Now we have inflation!

What happens to your investments? During inflationary times bond prices fall and yields on bonds increase. Because money buys less and less, people tend to buy tangibles like gold and real estate, pushing up their prices.

How fast times can lead to good times. People don't like inflation. So the government is forced to do something about it. The government tackles it by increasing the interest rate.

When the interest rates are high, we buy less. Demand decreases and consequently prices come down. Inflation loses steam. If this is done carefully, inflation may come down but the demand for goods and services will be high enough to keep the economy growing at a healthy pace.

What happens to your investments? If both inflation and unemployment is controlled, we have a time of growth.

How Economic Conditions Change Over Time

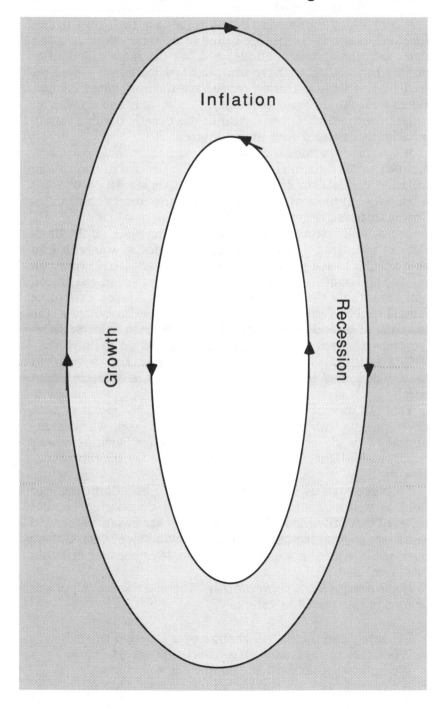

Everyone is relatively optimistic about the future and starts investing in the stock market. The stock market goes up.

A little bit of economics. Economists have their own names for these things. Bad times are called recessionary periods, good times are called growth periods, and fast times are called inflationary periods. As we have seen, each period contains its own seed of destruction. During recessions unemployment is high. When we try to decrease unemployment we may end up with an inflationary period. Growth periods are usually obtained when inflation is balanced with unemployment.

Why these periods cannot be predicted with accuracy. Nobody wants inflation or recession. The process of controlling inflation can lead to recession and vice versa. All of us want prosperity but most of the time we get either recession or inflation in different degrees of severity.

There are investing-affecting events taking place all the time. For example, Iran's need for more money for its war with Iraq compelled it to sell more and more oil; this resulted in other oil producing countries following suit, resulting in an overall oil glut. Inevitably the price of oil fell. Since the price of oil is critical to the Western economy, the lower price resulted in the lowering of several other costs; this was reflected in lower prices for many finished consumer goods. Inflation slowed down.

Odd as it may sound, among other things, Iran-Iraq might have contributed to the decline of inflation in Western countries!

That is precisely the problem. How to predict such developments with any degree of accuracy? Even when events appear to be closely connected to each other (such as money supply and inflation), it is not possible to predict the future consistently.

To make matters worse, many old "truths" don't seem to hold as well anymore. For example, for decades economists believed that inflation and unemployment are negatively related — as one goes up the other comes down and vice versa. But we have seen periods in which both unemployment and inflation have remained high.

What can we learn from all this? There are some important lessons in this for all investors:

- Economic conditions will change over a period of time.
- When they change, they affect our investments.
- We cannot predict how the conditions will change.
- We cannot predict when the conditions will change.

• Our investment program should take these realities into account.

The strategy for investing we are going to develop later takes into account the fact that the future is unpredictable.

Along the Way to Financial Freedom

Before we develop a strategy for investing, it is helpful to keep in mind certain basic principles. They may help you on your way to financial freedom. These principles are applicable to a variety of situations, even if you decide not to follow the strategy described here.

It is not what you make, but what you get to keep. There is a general tendency among most of us to concentrate more on what we make than on what we get to keep. Some of the money we make is fully taxed, some partly taxed and some not taxed at all. Whenever you make comparisons among investments, you should compare the after-tax returns.

For example, suppose your marginal tax rate (the tax you make on the last dollar you earn) is 30%. You are looking at
X. a taxable investment with a return of 10%, and
Y. a tax-free investment of 7.5%
Which should you choose?

Because you have to pay $30 on every $100 you earn on investment X, what you get to keep is only $70. On the other hand, in investment Y the $75 is yours to keep. Therefore, although 7.5% is lower than 10%, you should choose investment Y.

Another example: There are two mutual funds. Mutual fund "A" has an average return of 13% and mutual fund "B" has an average return of 15%. But to buy mutual fund "B", you have to pay a sales commission of 6%. Which one should you buy? The answer to this question is a little complex, but other things being equal, you are beter off with fund "A", unless you want to hold on to the fund for a long time.

Money you don't get to keep has no value to you. Concentrate on what you get to keep, no matter what the salespeople would like to have you believe.

Get rid of your debts. Debts prevent most people from getting rich. Debt is much more expensive than most people assume.

What is the real cost of borrowing?

Suppose you borrow $1,000 on your credit card. Your credit

charges may be $200 per year (this could be much higher). But this $200 has to come from your money after you have paid your taxes. This means that you have to earn much more than $200 to pay interest on your $1,000. If your marginal tax rate is 33% (federal and provincial combined), then you have to earn $300 to get an after-tax income of $200 (one-third or $100 goes to taxes). In other words, you are paying 30% interest in terms of your pre-tax income.

Take another example. Suppose you have a mortgage of $90,000, amortized over 25 years at 11%. How much interest would you have paid over the years? $169,830. If your marginal tax rate is 33% you would have to earn $254,745 or $10,189 per year just to pay the interest on your mortgage. Interest payments of over one-quarter of a million dollars on a $90,000 house! That's the real cost of getting into debt.

Are all debts bad? Not necessarily. Most of us have to get a mortgage to buy a house. But there are also ways of making money on borrowed money.

Yet, unless you are a professional, you should get rid of all debts as soon as possible. When you consider your debts, don't forget your mortgage!

If you must borrow, borrow for investing not for consumption. When you borrow for investing, the interest costs are tax deductible. When you borrow to buy a car, the interest payments cannot be deducted from your taxes. For example, suppose you have $15,000 worth of fully-paid investments. Now you would like to buy a car for $12,000. But if you buy the car on lease, the interest payments are not tax deductible. However, if you sell $12,000 worth of your investments to buy the car and then borrow $12,000 to invest, then the interest payment on the borrowed $12,000 is tax deductible.

Most people tend to buy consumer goods such as cars and boats using borrowed money while paying cash to buy investments. It should be the other way around.

Dollar cost averaging is an excellent way to buy. What is the best time to buy a stock, a mutual fund, gold or silver? To be frank, no one knows. An excellent strategy is to use dollar cost averaging. Dollar cost averaging is a technique of buying an investment on a regular basis resulting in a very advantageous overall price.

How does it work? You simply invest the same dollar amount in a given asset each month, quarter or year. For example, you want to buy gold but you do not know the best time to buy. Therefore you decide to invest $1,000 each year. Investing the same dollar amount has the following advantage: When the price is high you buy less; when the price is low you buy more. For example, if the price of gold is $500, you will be able to buy two ounces for $1,000; if the price of gold is $250, you will be able to buy four ounces for the same dollar amount. This is called dollar cost averaging.

To illustrate how this works, let us consider a stock XYZ in which you decide to invest $1,000 per year. Here is what happens:

Year	Price per share	No. shares bought	Amount
1978	$20	50	$ 1,000
1979	$15	67	$ 1,000
1980	$12	83	$ 1,000
1981	$10	100	$ 1,000
1982	$ 8	125	$ 1,000
1983	$ 5	200	$ 1,000
1984	$ 5	200	$ 1,000
1985	$ 5	200	$ 1,000
1986	$ 6	167	$ 1,000
1987	$ 8	125	$ 1,000
Total		1322	**$10,000**

In the above example, the investor has spent $10,000 to buy 1,322 shares. This works out to $7.54 per share. This is a remarkable result considering the investor paid more than this per share in six out of the ten years and the share is selling at less than half the original price! (This example is deliberately chosen to show that this technique works well even when a stock turns sour.)

Using dollar cost averaging will reduce your losses in declining markets and enhance your profits in a rising market.

Regular investing makes investing less risky. An effective way to invest is to be regular. For example, you may want to invest $200 every month. When you invest on a regular basis, several things happen. First, you are more aware of what your investments are doing. Second, because you are likely to invest about the same amount of money each month, you will be effectively dollar cost averaging. Third, what appears to be a small amount on a monthly basis can grow into a large sum over a long period. Fourth, you will not be tempted to spend the leftover money.

Each dollar you save and invest at the end of month will grow to an impressive amount over a period of time. For example, $1 saved each month and invested at 10% return will be worth $1,326 at the end of 25 years. In addition if you use techniques like dollar cost average and strategies like those described later, you would achieve financial freedom in a reasonable period of time.

The important thing in investing is to be disciplined and regular. It is even more important than the actual dollar amount you can save and invest.

Smart Investment Principles

- It is not what you make, it is what you get to keep
- Get rid of your debts
- If you must borrow, borrow for investing,
  not for consumption
- Dollar cost averaging is an excellent way to buy
- Regular investing makes investing less risky

In addition to all the things we discussed so far, we need a strategy, a blueprint for financial freedom. Such a strategy should protect us from temporary ups and downs in the market place. Without such a strategy, we will be at the mercy of the market and other external events. In the next few sections, we will discuss a strategy that is designed to achieve these goals.

II. FIRST LEG OF THE STRATEGY

East Pool/West Pool

In general, investments that are safe work slowly. Investments that are risky work fast. For example, you can buy Canada Savings Bonds which will almost certainly double your money in about eight years or you can buy a pork belly futures contract which may double your money in a week. The difference is that the chances of losing your money on CSBs are almost nil while the chances of losing your money on pork belly contracts are very high.

I am going to talk about getting rich slowly. But I also recognize that we should give ourselves some chance of getting there faster. So what should you do when you want to take a chance with a part of your money?

The best way is to build two pools of capital: East Pool and West Pool. The East Pool is your long-term nest egg. This part will make you financially independent in the long term no matter what. The West Pool, on the other hand, is an attempt to get rich quick or just to add some excitement to your life. You might lose everything in the West Pool, but you are not depending on it to become financially free.

How to Build the East Pool

The East Pool consists of conservative investments. The purpose of the East Pool is to lead you to financial independence in the long run. The main part of our strategy is to create and maintain the East Pool. We will deal with this in great detail later on.

When you start investing, or if you are a conservative investor by nature, all your money should be in this pool.

How to Build the West Pool

The West Pool consists of highly leveraged investments. There are no guarantees that you will make money with this pool, but when you do, it will be substantial. In this pool, you expect to win big; in the process, you may end up losing all the capital in this pool.

The West Pool is built from part of the money made in the East Pool. For example, suppose it is your objective to make 10% per year on the East Pool, but you make 18%. Now you have 8% more than you expected. This 8% is transferred to the West Pool and may be invested in more risky investments like options. If you make even more money on the West Pool, then transfer part of this money back to the East Pool.

East Pool/West Pool: An Example

Suppose you start with $20,000 in the East Pool, comprised of conservative investments. You expect to make 10% or $2,000 at the end of the year. But your investments have done better than you expected and you have made $4,000. Since this is $2,000 more than you expected to have, transfer the extra amount to the West Pool. Let us say that you decide to invest this money on options. Again assume that you do well and your options are later worth $5,000. You will return part of this money (say $2,500 to the East Pool) and continue to speculate with the remaining $2,500 in the West Pool.

East Pool / West Pool Strategy

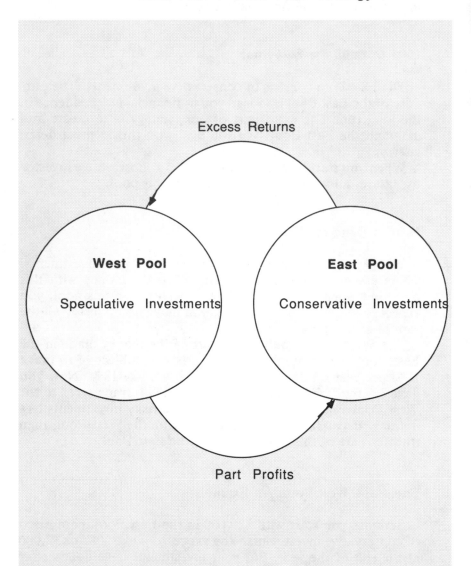

But what if your options do not make any money and you lose the $2,000 you invested? Well, you still have $22,000 in your East Pool and you have already achieved your minimum goal of making 10% for the year.

Simply put, the East Pool-West Pool Strategy gives you a chance to get rich faster, once you achieve your minimum goal each time.

III. SECOND LEG OF THE STRATEGY

RIGging the East Pool

Conservative Investments: Are There Any?

The East Pool has all your "conservative" investments. But what are conservative investments? Bonds? Stocks? Gold? Cash?

If you buy bonds, they will go down in value when the interest rate goes up. If you buy stocks, they will go down when there is a recession. If you buy gold, it may go down or stay at the same level when the economy grows. In fact almost any investment you can think of will go up or down in value depending on the economic conditions.

In other words, there are no universal conservative investments that will make money at all times. Different investments do well under different economic conditions.

Can We Predict the Future?

I just said that your investment's success depends on the economic conditions. Obviously we would all like to be able to predict the future so that we can all make the right investment decisions.

Who has seen the future? Many economists, forecasters, self-proclaimed gurus of gloom-and-doom tell us that they know what is going to happen to the economy. But do they really?

Here is a sampler of expert opinions:

A few years ago, *The Harvard Business Review* analyzed the predictions of 44 leading economists and forecasting organizations over a period of eight years. It concluded that almost everyone analyzed had been wrong some of the time.

David Dremen analyzed 52 surveys of expert forecasts between 1929 and 1980. In 77% of these surveys the experts did worse than the market average.

Mark Hulbert of *Hulbert Financial Digest* tracks the performance of over 75 newsletters. Only a handful of them give returns in excess of the market or even the safe T-bill rates.

Dr. Henry Kaufman is a well-respected economist and is paid well over one million dollars per year for his work. Yet, according to *Business Week,* his predictions have been frequently wrong. An analysis shows that, of his 12 major predictions, five were wrong!

Dr. Morton Shulman, a well-known Canadian investment advisor who claims a "batting average of 999", gave this advice in 1980 to the "widow class": Put about 50% of your money in gold and gold-related investments. He further predicted confidently that, five years down the road, no one following his advice "will regret it." Five years later gold was selling at 55% of its 1980 average price.

Joe Granville predicted that on September 28, 1981 the stock market would crash and it would be termed "blue Monday". On that day the market (DJI) soared 18 points, the highest one-day increase in six months!

I hope that I have convinced you that no one has the crystal ball, one that is any good anyway. True, there are experts who have predicted the future. The fact is that such predictions have not been consistent. The fact that someone has been spectacularly correct several times does not guarantee that he will be right the next time.

Different people have been correct at different times: Joe Granville has predicted the market with impressive results; Morton Shulman has picked stocks that have done extremely well; Kaufman has forecasted interest rates with great precision; the Aden sisters have predicted the gold market with extraordinary accuracy. Even I have been right at times.

The snag is that their predictions have hardly been consistent. They have also made spectacular mistakes, several more times than they care to remember or admit. If you doubt this, pick any (yes, any) newsletter or investment adviser. Ignore their claims, distorted statistics, selective presentation and hype. Go back five years and follow all that they have said in print over this period. You will quickly discover that there is no way you could have become rich following all their advice. You could have made a lot of money following some of their advice, but you could have also become bankrupt following some of their other advice.

Is there any exception to the above rule? Is there a Santa? Is there anyone who is consistently good at predicting the future? The answer is that maybe there is. But I personally do not know of any. (For the record, I read several thousand pages of investment information and advice every year, attend several investment conferences and am familiar with many investment advisers. All I can say is I am not any the wiser and "I came out of the same door wherein I went.")

Diversification Protects You Against an Uncertain Future

So if you accept that we cannot predict the future, how do we invest conservatively? After all, what is a conservative investment in inflationary times is not a conservative investment in recessionary times.

One way to protect ourselves against all possibilities is to diversify our investments such that when one investment goes down in value, some other investment that we hold might do well. But some questions come to mind:

1. What is diversification? If we randomly buy different investments are we diversified? Should we use a method to diversify our investments?

2. If we simply diversify, what good is it if all we do is to compensate the loss in one investment with gain in another? Is not the purpose of investing to get ahead rather than just compensating for potential loss?

The answer to the first set of questions is that haphazardly buying different investments is not proper diversification. For example, if you buy gold, silver, real estate, art and other such investments, you may face a heavy loss in recessionary times, even though you think you have "diversified" your investments. The answer to the second set of questions is that proper diversification should not only protect your investments, but it should also help you to get ahead.

In the next few sections we shall discuss how we can diversify properly and how to get ahead no matter what happens in the future. We start with a few rules to achieve our purpose.

Rule No. 1: Diversify with a purpose. As we discussed earlier, our diversification should have a purpose. In other words, if some of our investments go down in value, other investments we hold should go up in value. How do we assure ourselves that this is going to happen? Although there are several techniques by which this can be done, I am going to describe a strategy that I use. I call it RIGging.

RIGging is a way of diversifying your investments so that no matter what happens to the economy, you come out ahead.

What can happen to the economy in the future?

Earlier we saw that one of three things will happen to the economy:

1. Recession (Bad times)
2. Inflation (Fast times)
3. Growth/Prosperity (Good times)

Therefore, we can diversify to take care of the three economic conditions: (R)recession, I(inflation) and G(growth), or RIG for short. In other words, we will have some investments that will grow in value during recessionary periods, some that will grow in value during inflationary periods, and others that will grow during the growth period. Later on, we will see exactly how to do this.

Rule No. 2: Choose investments that will be sensitive to economic changes. Although each one of your investments will be affected by economic conditions, you want to choose investments that will be very sensitive to economic change. This is because you don't just want to balance your investments but to actually increase their value. Therefore it makes sense to have investments that will rise quickly during each economic period.

Rule No. 3: Rearrange your investments from time to time to take advantage of the investments that are less favoured. For example, during a growth period the price of stocks that you hold may have doubled. At the same time, the price of gold (which is an inflation-oriented investment) may have gone down in value. It may now be worthwhile to sell some of your stocks to buy gold. By doing this, you take some of the profit from a currently high-priced investment (stocks) and buy a currently disfavoured and low-priced investment (gold) that will increase in value under different economic conditions.

How to Diversify Your Investments

1. Diversify with a purpose
2. Choose investments that are sensitive to economic changes
3. Rearrange your investment mix from time to time

These are the basic principles. From now on we are going to discuss how to use these principles to build the East Pool.

Setting Up the East Pool: An Example

To understand the principles better, let me assume that you have $30,000 to begin with and you can add $300 per month. The amount of money is not important here — you may have only $10,000 or just $3,000 to begin with; it does not matter.

As we see, different investments do well at different times. In Chart 7, we identify each investment as R(recession), I(inflation) or G(growth) type. If you look through the charts, you will see that bonds and cash equivalents are R-type investments, real estate and gold are I-type investments and common stocks and real estate are G-type investments. Therefore you want to own some of each type of investment.

Winners and Losers Under Different Conditions

Economic Condition	Winners	Losers
Recession	Bonds Cash Equivalents	Real Estate Precious Metals Antiques/Collectibles Common Stocks
Inflation	Real Estate Gold	Cash Equivalents Common Stocks (Bonds)
Growth	Common Stocks Real Estate	Bonds Cash Equivalents Collectibles Precious Metals

Some Common Investments and Their Types (Chart 7)

Investment	Type
Bonds	R
Cash	R
Cash Equivalents	R
Common Stocks	G
Gold	I
Real Estate	I/G

But how much of each? That would depend on your expectations. But if you are like me, you might simply say that you do not have any idea as to what is going to happen in the future. Therefore, you would invest equally in all three kinds of investments. This means that you would divide $30,000 into three equal parts and invest $10,000 in R-type investments, $10,000 in I-type investments and $10,000 in G-type investments.

Let us assume that you decide to use mutual funds for implementing your strategy. Then you may want to buy $10,000 worth of precious metals and real estate funds (I-type), $10,000 worth of equity funds (G-type) and $10,000 worth of bond and mortgage funds (R-type). Now you have intelligently diversified your investments.

Each month, you could invest the same amount in each type of investment. If you save $300 per month, then you could add $100 to each type. (Or, alternatively, you could add a certain amount to I-type one month and a similar amount to G-type the following month and to R-type the month after.) By doing this, you are dollar cost averaging your purchases.

At the end of each year, you review your investments. In the above example, you started with $10,000 for each type of investment and added $100 per month. By the end of the year you have contributed:

$11,200 for I-type mutual funds
$11,200 for G-type mutual funds
$11,200 for R-type mutual funds
($33,600 in total)

However, depending on the economic conditions some of your investments would have gone down and some would have gone up. Calculate the current value of your investments. Suppose it looks like this:

The current value of I-type mutual funds: $ 9,900
The current value of G-type mutual funds: $16,800
The current value of R-type mutual funds: $12,300
Total   **$39,000**

During the year, G-type investments have appreciated in value and I-type have gone down. At this point, I-type investments are cheaper relative to G-type investments. Therefore, it would make sense to take some profits from G-type investments and buy more I-type investments. In other words, we want to accumulate investments that are cheaper now because we know that when the economic conditions change we will benefit by this move. Therefore at the end of the year we rearrange our portfolio so that once again we have the same amount in each type of investment:
$13,000 for I-type mutual funds
$13,000 for G-type mutual funds
$13,000 for R-type mutual funds
($39,000 in total)

Although at this stage we have the same dollar amount in each type of investment, we have more units of I-type investments. We obtained these by selling some of our G-type investments. In other words, we are selling high and buying low.

During the following year, we continue to invest a similar amount in each type of investment. At the end of the year, we re-adjust such that each type of investment has the same dollar amount.

This strategy is summarized in the "Three-Step Investment" chart.

Three-Step Investment Strategy for the East Pool

Step: 1: Your Start-up
Divide your money into three equal parts and invest it in three different types of investments (R, I and G). If you invest on a regular basis, invest equally in these three types of investments.

Starting Position (example)
Type R: $$$$$$$$$$$ $11,200
Type I: $$$$$$$$$$$ $11,200
Type G: $$$$$$$$$$$ $11,200

Step 2: Review
Calculate the value of your three types of investments at least once a year and whenever you think the value of one type of investment has gone up or down sharply.

Year-end Market Change Review (example)
Type R:	$$$$$$$$$$$	$ 9,900
Type I:	$$$$$$$$$$$$$	$12,300
Type G:	$$$$$$$$$$$$$$$$$$$	$16,800

Step 3: Adjustment
If the value of one of your investments is at least 20% lower or higher than the others, readjust your portfolio so that each type of investment has roughly the same value.

Adjustment (example)
Type R:	$$$$$$$$$$$$$$	$13,000
Type I:	$$$$$$$$$$$$$$	$13,000
Type G:	$$$$$$$$$$$$$$	$13,000

Continue investing consistently following the above three steps.

Although for the sake of convenience we rearrange investments once a year, there is nothing magical about the year-end. Any time you feel that there is an imbalance (say about 20% difference in value between the value of any two types of investments), you may rearrange the portfolio. Conversely, at the year-end if there is no major difference in value among the three investment types, you may want to leave the investments as they are until the next year or until a major imbalance develops.

That is all there is to building the East Pool.

The East Pool is also flexible. You can add money to the pool any time. If you think that inflation is around the corner, you may want to readjust the portfolio and give greater weight to I-type investments. If you do not want to predict, you may follow the example above. If you do not like to invest in mutual funds, you can choose your own investments as long as you diversify as mentioned above.

The East Pool Technique: Why Does it Work?

The East Pool strategy incorporates several ideas. Although it appears simple and mechanical, it incorporates several sound investment ideas. These are described below.

The East Pool is hedged. One reason why the East Pool technique will work is that it is based on the hedge principle. For example, whenever the real interest rates are high, the price of gold is low; whenever the real interest rates are low, the price of gold is high. If you buy both gold and bonds, then as one goes down, the other goes up. Therefore you are protected no matter what happens. The RIGging technique counterbalances your portfolio with investments that work in different directions at any given time.

The East Pool buys low, sells high. Your East Pool buys low by using two techniques: dollar cost averaging and RIG balancing. When the RIG investments are readjusted periodically, we are in fact selling part of the investments that have appreciated in value and buying investments that are relatively undervalued. Thus we buy low and sell high.

Suppose we buy 1,000 shares of a stock fund at $10 each and 1,000 shares of a gold fund at $10 each. If at the end of the year our stock fund is worth $13 per unit and the gold fund is worth $9 per unit. Your stock shares are now worth $13,000 and the gold shares are worth $9,000. Now, if you sell $2,000 worth of stock fund shares (2,000/$13 = 153.8 shares) and buy gold fund shares (2,000/$9 = 222 shares) you will have fewer stock fund shares and more gold fund shares, although the market value of both types is the same.

When economic conditions change and the gold fund shares start going up and stock funds start going down, you have more gold fund shares and fewer stock fund shares. In other words your profit potential is increased and your loss potential is controlled.

The East Pool provides for all major possibilities. The East Pool strategy is designed to cover all major economic conditions. Although no one can predict the future, from an investment point of view the strategy covers a complete spectrum of events. Therefore, you do not have to second-guess the mind of the market to become financially free.

IV. THIRD LEG OF THE STRATEGY

Speculating With the West Pool

The heart of our strategy is creating and maintaining the East Pool. For most people it is not necessary (or even desirable) to speculate. But if you would like to speculate, then you may want to create the West Pool for this purpose.

How to Create the West Pool

The West Pool is created through profits made in the East Pool. First, you should start with some minimum objective for the East Pool. For example, you may decide that you want your money to grow at least 8% each year. Therefore, if you start with $10,000 in the East Pool, at the end of the year you would expect it to be at least $10,800. Instead, if the value of your East Pool investments stands at $12,000, you have $1,200 more ($12,000-$10,800) than your target. This extra cash is transferred to the West Pool. It is this spare cash — $1,200 — that you use to speculate.

What to do With the Money in the West Pool

As we noted earlier, speculative investments such as options, penny stocks, venture capital or commodity futures are high-risk/high-reward in nature. When you invest in them either you will multiply your money quickly or lose it equally quickly.

Let us assume that you invest your money in commodity options and make 200% profit in three months. Now your West Pool is worth $3,600. At this stage, you should strengthen the East Pool by investing part of the profit there. Thus, you may decide to put $1,800 in the East Pool and continue to speculate with the remaining $1,800.

In this example, the East Pool provided the money for the West Pool and the West Pool, in turn, increased the total worth of the East Pool. Thus each pool can be used to strengthen the other.

But it should not be assumed that the West Pool will always make money. It is quite likely that you end up losing all your initial West Pool investment of $1,200. When this happens, you have to wait until you achieve your next year's target on the East Pool. Because the West Pool is created after your minimum objective has been achieved on the East Pool, even if you lose all your money in the West Pool, you should still be able to do well in the long run.

Should You Have a West Pool At All?

Generally speaking, specualation is not a game for beginners. Intelligent speculation requires a great deal of preparation and a cunning ability to predict human behaviour ... and a lot of luck. Anything less and you are sure to lose 100% of your investment (and even more if you are not careful).

No one but you can answer the question of whether you should speculate. There are two guidelines: first, don't speculate if you are not prepared to lose all; and second, don't speculate with money you should be devoting to a conservative long-term strategy (the East Pool). Normally, you should put no more than 20% of your money into speculation and very little money into high-risk speculation.

Rules of the Wild West

Most people don't realize that the rules for speculating are very different from those for investing. In fact, the rules of speculation may contradict the rules of long-term investing. Here are some "rules" of speculation:

Don't speculate with trivial amounts. When you're investing, no amount is really too small. Every little bit helps. Speculation is different. Because intelligent speculation takes sure preparation and effort, it's not worth your while to speculate with small amounts of money. If you speculate with $100 and make $500, you are still poor. It is not worthwhile taking chances with your money, if even when you win it is hardly going to make any difference to your life. The purpose of speculation is to give yourself a chance that will make a difference. Trivial amounts cannot do this. Therefore, small amounts are for investing, not for speculating.

Don't diversify. Speculation needs both knowledge and discipline. The market is enormously complicated and just one corner of it is challenge enough. Small investors especially should concentrate their energy and resources on specific speculative investments. Diversification of speculative investments needs considerable resources and knowledge and is best left to specialists and full-time traders.

Cut your losses early. You should be prepared for ups and downs while speculating. But the West Pool is not for the long haul. If the market moves unexpectedly against you and if your losses reach a certain predetermined level, quit. Your objective in the West Pool is to be in the game as long as possible. There will always be other opportunities.

Take your profits soon. In speculative markets profits can quickly turn into losses. In today's complex market there are ways in which you can lock in your profits at different levels (e.g., buying a put option to protect the profits made in a futures contract). But, if you do not use sophisticated strategies, quit while you are ahead. Nobody sells at the top of the market. Don't let greed turn profits into losses.

Try to predict the future. Speculation is the art of second-guessing human nature and the future of the economy. It's the action of investors that causes the market's ebb and flow. To speculate successfully, you need to be a student of human nature and economics and to understand the many factors that impinge on the rise and fall of stocks, bonds, commodities, real estate, art and collectibles. Then you can make intelligent guesses.

How to Speculate Right

- Don't speculate with trivial amounts
- Don't diversify
- Cut your losses early
- Take your profits soon
- Try to predict the future

No One Can Guarantee Success When You Speculate

Even if you follow all the above rules of speculation, there is still no guarantee of success. That's why you should not set up a West Pool unless you are willing to lose. If, even after reading all this, you would still like to set up a West Pool, I would suggest that you read at least one good book on the art of speculation. My favourite is *The Zurich Axioms: The Investment Secrets of Swiss Bankers* by Max Gunther (Published by the New American Library, New York, 1985).

V. PUTTING IT ALL TOGETHER

"The Compleat Strategist"

Getting rich quickly is not a realistic goal for most of us. But getting rich slowly is within the grasp of most of us. To achieve financial freedom you need time, discipline, knowledge and strategy. To review some principles of investing that you may want to keep in mind:

- It is not what you make that counts, it is what you get to keep.
- Get rid of all your debts.
- If you must borrow, borrow for investing and not for consumption.
- Dollar cost averaging is an excellent way to buy.
- Regular investing makes investing less risky.

Different investments do well under different conditions. Therefore, it is wise to invest in different investments so that irrespective of the economic condition — be it inflation, recession or growth — we have scope to make money.

The strategy suggested here is to divide your money into three parts and invest in R-type, I-type and G-type investments. Whenever major profits are generated in any one of these three types of investments, we can invest part of the profits into a type that is not currently doing well. By following this strategy on a regular basis, you can achieve financial freedom while at the same time protecting yourself against economic cycles.

If you want to speculate, you should create a different pool of funds made up of some of the profits made through the strategy suggested in the previous paragraphs. By swapping excess funds between conservative and speculative portfolios, it is possible to achieve financial freedom, even if our speculative investments fail to do well in the long run.

Financial freedom means different things to different people. The strategy described here is based on the assumption that you are financially free if you can have income from your investments that is as large as your salary. If you start relatively young and save 10% of your income regularly, this is a very realistic goal.

The concepts developed in this article arise out of the work of several people. Some concepts such as dollar cost averaging have been known for a long time. Others such as the East-West Pool and diversifying against different economic outcomes arise out of the concepts developed by investment experts such as Ira Cobleigh, Bruce Dorfman and Harry Browne. Although I have used some of their concepts, I have refrained from mentioning their names directly. This is because I have changed the concepts substantially and my exposition does not necessarily represent their initial ideas. Yet I would like to acknowledge their influence on my thinking without in any way implying that I am representing their concepts.

CHAPTER 4

INVESTING IN REAL ESTATE

By Keith Laushway

INTRODUCTION

The objective of this chapter is to provide a basic introduction to investing in real estate. The chapter is directed to the "weekend investor", the person who is considering investing in real estate on a part-time basis and is wondering where to start. It is also directed to the person who may have already invested in a property or two and has now decided to begin "reading the instructions". For these people, the information contained in this chapter should either provide some confirmation of what they have done or suggest things they might have done differently.

This chapter will not provide a technical explanation of the mechanical in's and out's of real estate investing such as analyzing purchase and sale agreements, discussing problems on the closing of a deal, or the wording of partnership agreements. In most cases these and other similar types of problems are unique to a particular investment and the new real estate investor should be discussing these issues with his or her professional real estate broker, lawyer or financial advisor.

This chapter does provide a general framework for investing in real estate. It examines some of the advantages and disadvantages of real estate as an investment. It looks at the questions of how to find a real estate investment, and how much to pay for it once you have found it. Basic financial concepts such as leveraging are discussed and sources of financing and general tax issues are outlined. It looks at whether you should invest alone or with others and at the different types of group investing. Finally, the characteristics or different types of real estate investments, from land development to office buildings, are examined.

SETTING THE SCENE

Advantages and Disadvantages of Real Estate as an Investment

Every type of investment has its good and bad side. Real estate is no exception. Because we are so familiar with real estate — it surrounds us constantly and we have heard so many success stories about people who have invested in it — we have a tendency to overlook the disadvantages which are peculiar to this type of investment. So, before taking the plunge, it might be a good idea to remind ourselves of these disadvantages and then get on to the special advantages.

Disadvantages

Large Capital Requirement. Compared to other types of investments, real estate requires a large capital commitment. If you are starting small and borrowing as much of the purchase price as is safely possible you will still need anywhere from $10,000 to $50,000 of your own money in today's real estate markets. Stocks and bonds, on the other hand, can be purchased for less than $1,000. Because of the relatively low capital requirements for these types of investments, a reasonably diversified portfolio of stocks and bonds can be purchased for $10,000 to $15,000. A diversified portfolio of stocks and bonds will spread the risk that any one of them will go sour. Real estate, however, is not something the average investor can diversify. Acquisitions of real estate, because of their size, usually occur one at a time over long periods. The consequences of making a poor investment on one property can be quite severe.

Lack of Liquidity. An investment's liquidity is a measure of the ability to turn that investment into cash without losing the value of the investment. Most investments suffer liquidity problems from time to time.

It may be that what you have to sell is just not in favour at some particular time. If so, it will take a long time to sell it and you will probably have to sell at a loss. Real estate is a particularly illiquid investment. Unless you happen to be in the middle of an active market where your property is in demand it could take anywhere from a few weeks to a year or more to sell your property. Even a quick sale generally results in a three to six week period between the time an offer is accepted and the time the deal closes and you receive your money.

Instead of selling, you could try to raise the required cash by refinancing your property if you have equity built up in it. The refinancing could take the form of new first mortgage terms or a second mortgage. However, the lender in these circumstances would still normally require at least a week or two to approve such requests.

Before embarking on a real estate investment program you should carefully consider your future cash needs and build in a few contingencies so that you are not forced to sell your property at a low price just to meet these needs.

Long Holding Period. Unless you are engaged in speculating on quick flips of property, investing in real estate is seldom done in anticipation of short-term profits. As a rule, medium to long-term returns are expected mainly from the appreciating value of the property. The longer holding period required of real estate gives rise to many uncertainties. Who knows whether or how a neighbourhood will change over your expected holding period. Perhaps five years from now the type of property you have bought will no longer be in favour or will become obsolete.

It is not possible to eliminate the risks associated with a long holding period. However, these risks can be minimized by carefully analyzing the type and location of the property you are thinking of buying in an attempt to anticipate its future use. Then, once you have bought it, you must continually monitor the property to see if there are any reasons why your conclusions about its use would change.

Exposure to Government Control. Real estate is particularly vulnerable to government laws and regulations. All levels of government are interested in influencing the use of property. Building codes, planning and zoning requirements, environmental impact regulations, and rent controls are just a few of the ongoing governmental influences on the use of real estate. In addition, governments have the power to enforce building moratoria, condemnation orders, and expropriation proceedings. Changes in governments' attitudes towards the particular use of a property could seriously alter an investor's expected return from that property. Such attitudes must be constantly monitored by a real estate investor.

Lack of Standardization. Some types of investments are easier to compare than others, making it easier to identify good buys and bad buys. Real estate is at the bottom of the list in this category. No two pieces of real estate property are the same. Two buildings may look identical but they have had different histories. Tenants and owners were different, as was upkeep and maintenance. The locations of the buildings are different. Even seemingly similar buildings that sit side-by-side or across the street from each other could have a value component determined by their relative locations.

This lack of standardization makes it very difficult to precisely value a property. Valuation techniques may give a reasonable estimate; however, there is usually a large judgemental element involved.

This risk of making a poor decision can be reduced by doing your homework in terms of comparing the property you would like to buy to as many other similar properties as possible, noting the characteristics of your target property. Until you feel confident about your own judgement in these matters you should use experts such as real estate brokers, appraisers, architects and contractors.

Subjective Feelings. There are investors who refuse to part with the stock of a company or a bond certificate because it was the first investment they made, or the stock or bond was left in a will, or simply because the certificate is beautiful. We might chuckle about this. However, watch out. Real estate investors, especially new ones, are susceptible to making subjective (meaning emotional) decisions about which property they want to buy. Think about the last house you bought for yourself and your family to live in. You were not just buying bricks, wood and plaster. You were buying a home, a place to raise a family, a lifestyle, a dream. You were willing to pay as much as you could afford and then some, for all of these things. A lot of this emotionalism can get carried over into real estate investment decisions. Many people would rather own an attractive investment property in a nice neighbourhood even if it will produce less of a return than a run-down building in an undesirable area of town.

Work. Real estate investing is hard work. There are constant demands on your time, energy and money. It is the equivalent of holding down a part-time job. You are either always looking for property, maintaining the property you own, worrying about the property you own, or trying to sell property. You can put your money into some investments and forget about them until you get your interest or dividend cheque. Real estate investing is not like that, and unless you are willing to accept its special demands you will have a difficult time doing it successfully.

Advantages

Now that we have seen the disadvantages let's look at the other side of the scale and examine the advantages.

A Basic Soundness. Many of the world's great private fortunes are based on property investment. In many cases if the fortune is not based on real estate there are at least substantial real estate holdings. The reason for this is that there is a basic stability in real estate as an investment. Other types of investments may fall out of favour and become worthless over time but real estate always seem to have some value. It has been one of the most consistent investments in man's commercial history.

This basic soundness does not mean that you can go out and pick any piece of property and expect to make a fortune. It does mean that if you carefully select your property you will usually at least succeed in preserving your capital, and the preservation of capital is the number one investment rule. Even when you have chosen poorly or have just experienced plain bad luck, chances are that you will not lose as great a percentage of your capital investing in real estate as you would investing in something else.

Limited Supply. It's a basic fact of life that the real estate pie is not getting bigger. The world supply of land is fixed. The world demand for land is increasing as the population increases. These facts must operate together to force land values to increase over time relative to other products and services where the supply is not fixed. However, land values do not increase uniformly in place or time. Increases would be more pronounced in large populated centres than in rural communities, and there are increases and decreases in value dependent on economic cycles and community life cycles. But over the long run the value of most carefully selected property goes up.

Investment Objectives

The single most important thing you can do before you spend any of your money on real estate is to set out your real estate investing goals — what kind and how much of a return do you want, what level of risk are you willing to accept, what kind of property do you want, where do you expect to be two years from now, three years, five years and so on.

Winning at anything requires an objective, a plan for

reaching that objective, and a constant evaluation of the implementation of that plan. All successful people do this, all successful companies do this, all successful sports teams do this. Real estate investing is no different. Failure to set goals in real estate is like buying a car off a car lot with your eyes shut. The style, colour, use and price may be totally unsuited to your needs. A real estate investment suited to a young person starting out on his or her career, with little capital, few obligations and lots of time will be considerably different from the type of real estate investment suited to a person who is well advanced in his or her career, has a family, more capital, less time, and is in a higher tax bracket.

When setting your goals several factors should be considered, including your age, lifestyle, available capital, risk-taking nature, requirements for cash flow and so on. The goals cannot be set in isolation without considering the rest of your financial planning objectives. If you cannot do this type of planning yourself you may have to seek the help of professionals in setting your overall investment portfolio goals and placing real estate investing within the context of those goals.

Some of the more common real estate investment objectives are listed below.

Protection of Capital. Many real estate investors, especially new ones, have protection of capital as their highest priority. They want to invest in property where the risk of losing their initial investment stake is very low. The rational is that it takes too long to earn that initial stake to risk losing it in a speculative venture and have to start over again. It is better to build up capital first through conservative investments and then to branch out into riskier investments once you have built a strong base.

The most conservative investments are found in quality rental properties with quality tenants, in a good location. Of course, there is a price to pay for choosing safety first — you must sacrifice the opportunity for a high rate of return.

Appreciation. If you buy a property for $150,000 and sell it for $175,000 you have realized your return in the form of an appreciation in the value of the property of $25,000. Some investors prefer to realize their profits only in the form of appreciation over a period of time. This would occur where a property was producing little or no net income during the period it was owned and the entire return was dependent on the sale price. The most common example of property purchased for its appreciation is raw land.

Earnings. Some investors' main concern is that the property they have purchased is capable of producing a steady stream of net income after all the expenses of operating the property have been deducted from the rental revenue received. Many investors achieve this goal by purchasing a rental property and then upgrading that property to attract better tenants who are willing to pay higher rents than the previous tenants.

Liquidity. If you want to be able to sell your property quickly, easily, and without a loss you will be looking for a property with a high degree of liquidity. Liquidity is difficult to find in real estate investments since by nature real estate is not sold quickly or easily unless you are willing to take a loss. Liquidity does not come cheaply. You will likely have to accept a lower rate of return in order to achieve it since liquidity is rare and attractive to other investors.

Freedom From Work or Worry. If this is your goal it's unlikely that you will find it in the real estate industry. You might be better off choosing a blue chip stock or a Canada Savings Bond.

Tax Shelters. Many investors try to use Federal income tax laws to produce non-taxable income through investing in real estate. In certain cases this can be done. However, real estate has a greater reputation in this area than it deserves. If this is your objective, the best place to start is by consulting a tax expert to find out the latest developments in this area.

Once your goals are set, you can then examine the many types of property in your area to see which property can satisfy those goals. At some stage you will probably have to contact a real estate professional in order to ask questions about specific properties that relate to your objectives. After your goals are set it becomes easier to eliminate properties and concentrate only on those that relate to what you want to achieve. Those properties that are left should be analyzed in terms of the building, the site, the location, and the general business and real estate market to see what impact these elements will have on your objectives. For example, if achieving a capital appreciation is your primary objective, then the location of the property is relatively more important than the building on the property. You would want to find property in an area which is experiencing new growth and purchase raw land, or find an area which is being rejuvenated and purchase a building for renovation and sale.

HOW TO FIND IT AND WHAT TO DO WITH IT WHEN YOU HAVE FOUND IT

Where to Look and What to Look For

You have decided that real estate is for you. You have set your objectives. You know the type of property you want. You know approximately how much you can afford to pay. Now what do you do? How do you find the property?

Finding a good property will probably be the single most difficult part of real estate investing. Unless you have had plenty of experience and know what you are doing (in which case you do not need the information in this chapter) do not rush out and buy the first property you stumble across. You could get lucky and buy a winner — but more likely you will end up paying too much for a loser. Take your time, look around, try to develop a feel for what has potential value and what does not. If you miss an opportunity by taking slow steps at first there will be others, and you will more than likely avoid costly mistakes.

As with most endeavours, the best way to start is to try to get a broad picture of what is happening in the real estate market in your chosen area. It is usually preferable to start in your own backyard. You are already familiar with it. You will hear about opportunities, read about zoning changes, hear on the news about property disputes, government plans, bad areas, good areas and so on. Unless you live in a depressed economy it is unlikely that the grass will be much greener in someone else's backyard. As you gain experience and capital you can consider opportunities that are further afield.

The best place to start looking is in the real estate advertisements in your local newspapers. You should look to see what kinds of property are for sale, where they are located and the price. Newspaper advertisements are a prime source for this type of information. In addition to local newspapers, your area may have a locally-published real estate news service which deals exclusively with real estate listings.

Once you have an idea of what the market is like from real estate ads and you have noted the more promising properties, you should go out and drive around the various neighbourhoods, paying particular attention to their individual characteristics. You should try to match these characteristics to the ones desired by potential users of the property. For example, is there adequate accessibility to major thruways for retail operations? Are there nuisances in a residential neighbourhood, such as sports stadiums, late night clubs or smelly factories? How convenient is shopping, public transportation, schools or any other amenities required to make an area attractive to its users? What is the predominate use of property in the neighbourhood? It makes little sense to look for a residential rental building in an area that is turning into light industrial use.

If you are considering residential rental property, check the prevailing range of rents in the neighbourhood. You'll need to know the highest rents being charged so that you will not price yourself out of the market if you buy a place, upgrade it and increase rents.

By driving around various neighbourhoods you will soon eliminate many of them for one reason or another and will have an idea of the areas in which you should concentrate.

After you have decided that an area interests you and it's time to investigate it more thoroughly, you should find a good real estate broker who knows the area. A good broker can save you a lot of work answering the 101 questions you should be asking about any neighbourhood you want to invest in. When it comes time to look at specific properties a good broker can help you identify the properties with good value or from which good value can be realized by making a few upgrades. A word of caution about brokers should be mentioned. Unless your broker is a friend or unless the two of you have a longstanding professional relationship, do not automatically assume that your broker is always looking out for your best interests. The broker's job is to sell you property. The good ones will make your best interests their priority in order to retain your future business and to obtain referrals. Others may not.

Agents and brokers have access to up-to-date listings of properties that may not be listed in newspapers. Between the two sources, you should be able to make a comprehensive list of all the properties available for sale in any area that you would have an interest.

As with the best jobs, some of the best real estate is sold by vendors who did not advertise and who sometimes did not plan to sell. Word-of-mouth or a direct approach are responsible for such sales. Often someone will approach the owner of an attractive property and ask if it is for sale and if so how much would he sell it for. In such cases, the potential vendor may simply ask that an offer be made which will be considered. It takes a lot of work to find this kind of property, but it can be worthwhile.

Finally, as a potential purchaser you could place an advertisement in a newspaper saying what type of property you would like to buy and its location.

How Much To Pay

Valuing real estate is not an exact science. The problem is that no two parcels of real estate are exactly alike. The best you can hope for as a potential purchaser is an estimate of its value which you would then use as a basis for negotiations with the owner.

There are several methods used to arrive at a ballpark figure when valuing property. Three of the most common ones are discussed below. No one method is precise. No method should be totally relied upon to provide more than a framework for negotiations with a vendor and to help you establish a price beyond which you will say to yourself you would rather look for another property.

Comparison Method. This approach involves finding comparable properties that have been sold recently, finding out the sale price, making some adjustments to that sale price, and using the final number as a basic of comparison for the property you are looking at.

The comparison method is good for single family dwellings, condominiums and vacant land, mainly because these properties are more numerous, there are frequent sales, and they are more easily compared. However, adjustments must still be made to the sale price of a comparable property in order to get a better estimate of the value of your target property. For example, the location of the comparable property may be better or worse. The sale could have taken place six months ago in an active market. The circumstances of the sale, such as a forced sale, may have had an impact on the price. As can be seen, the comparison method can be very subjective. However, after comparing many property values you should get a general feel for the value of a particular property.

Cost Approach. The cost approach consists of estimating the cost of constructing a new building of comparable size and quality to the building you are considering. Add the cost of the land to this cost and compare the total to the asking price of the vendor of your target property.

To estimate the cost of constructing a new building, you would determine the square footage of the target building and then check with a real estate broker or a contractor to get an estimate of the cost of constructing a building of similar quality. If the target building is not new, you should make an adjustment for its depreciated value. All buildings have an estimated useful life beyond which it becomes impractical to maintain or repair them. The adjustment for any particular building would depend on its estimated useful life, its age, and how well maintained it has been. This is a difficult adjustment to make and will probably require professional assistance.

The land value would be estimated using the comparison approach discussed earlier. The sale price of several vacant lots in the area with potential uses similar to your target property should be examined and adjustments made for such things as location, size and use.

The cost approach can be used to estimate the value of any property. However, it is most often used to value property which is not sold very often and is not purchased for investment purposes, such as public buildings, schools, hospitals, etc.

Income Approach. The income approach is the basic approach used when purchasing investment or income property.

Whenever you purchase an income property you are really buying a stream of income that stretches into the future and includes the selling price of that property. The question becomes: what would you pay for an expected stream of income from a particular property? If you wanted an average return of 15% per year for the risk of investing in a particular property, and the property was producing $15,000 of income per year with very little potential for profit when resold, then you would not pay more than $100,000 for that property ($15,000 ÷ $100,000 = 15%). If the income from that property was only $10,000 per year rather than $15,000 per year, you would have to have a reasonable expectation that the eventual sale price would produce a profit large enough to bring the average yearly return up to 15% before you would pay $100,000 for that property. As can be seen, the analysis of the yearly income stream, of an investment property is very important unless you are buying property solely for capital appreciation.

When analyzing the future income stream, the figure that is usually most important is the annual income before interest costs and taxes. It is only after you have determined this number that you can decide whether the income earned by the property will support the borrowing costs you must incur to buy the property and whether the overall expected net return after taxes makes the whole venture worthwhile. To get to this point, several intermediate steps must be taken.

Determine Adjusted Gross Rental Income. Examine the books and accounting records kept for the property for the current and past few years to get a picture of the income generated during that time and to form a basis for expected future rental revenue.

For residential property controlled by rent review legislation check to see what the maximum rent increases can be. If the property is a commercial investment check the tenant leases very carefully. These leases are your investment.

After you have an idea of what to expect in terms of gross annual rent, you should deduct an allowance for vacancies. To do this you would examine the historical vacancy rate of the building, assess the future anticipated market vacancy for the type of building you are considering and come to a realistic number for the future.

It will also be necessary to make an allowance for bad debts — i.e., tenants who move out without paying their rent.

Net Income Before Interest Costs And Taxes. From the adjusted gross rental income deduct estimated operating expenses, repairs and maintenance and fixed expenses to arrive at net income before interest and taxes.

Operating expenses are those normal expenses required for the day-to-day operation of the property, such as janitorial services and management. These types of expenses usually fluctuate with the level of occupancy. If the building is 100% occupied these expenses would be at their highest. As the occupancy decreases, these expenses have a tendency to decrease.

Repairs and maintenance involve the upkeep of the property from repainting an apartment after a tenant has moved out to repairing staircases. These expenses tend to increase as tenant turnover increases.

Fixed expenses are those which do not change regardless of the vacancy rate of a building. Whether a building is full or empty, expenses such as insurance and property taxes must still be paid. After these expenses have been deducted from the adjusted gross rental income, the balance left is net income before interest costs and taxes.

Required Rate Of Return. You should now determine what rate of return you expect for taking the risk of investing in that property. While the determination of the expected rate of return is very subjective, there are a few things to keep in mind. An overall expected rate of return is made up of several component parts.

The starting point is to determine the current and expected

riskless rate of return for the economy as a whole. If Government of Canada Treasury Bills, which are generally considered a riskless investment, are paying 10%, you should not be willing to accept a lower rate of return on a relatively riskier investment such as real estate. In fact you would expect a premium over and above the riskless rate of return. The size of this premium would depend on your evaluation of the riskiness of a property. The greater the risk, the greater the premium. The risk associated with investment property is that you will not earn what you expected to earn on the property because of the uncertainty surrounding the development of the area where the property is located, the general economy, or any number of other reasons.

In addition to a risk premium you would probably want a liquidity premium for putting your money into an investment that is difficult to turn into cash. The risk here is basically that you may have to confront a situation where you will be required to sell your property on short notice to raise cash to meet another emergency. This cannot normally be done unless the property is substantially discounted in value. To compensate you for accepting such a risk you would want to add a premium to the riskless rate of return.

Finally, there is a time, labour and attention premium. Because real estate requires a relatively large amount of time, labour and attention, you would want a premium over the riskless rate of return to compensate you for this additional work.

Once you have considered all of these factors you would add the various premiums to the riskless rate of return to find your own expected rate of return.

Naturally, none of this is done in isolation. You will also be shopping around the marketplace to see what the expected rates of return are on various properties similar to the property you are considering. This can be done by dividing the new income before interest costs and tax by the sale price of the property. There are some problems with this comparison approach since you will not know the full details behind the sale price. But if you look at enough properties you should get a good feel for what kind of return the market is expecting on a property. You would then compare the market return with the kind of return you would like, to see if your expected return is realistic or whether the market or your building is over- or under-priced.

Effect Of Borrowing. Once you have determined the expected rate of return before interest costs and taxes you can determine how much, if any, borrowed funds can be supported by the property and what effect the cost of these borrowed funds will have on the expected return.

Let's say that the expected annual cash flow after all expenses except interest and taxes is $10,000 on a $100,000 property, and that the expected annual average rate of return (before interest and taxes) by the time the property is sold is 13%. Assume also that you could borrow up to $75,000 at 12% to buy this property. Since the property is generating $10,000 per year it can support the $9,000 a year in interest that it would cost to borrow the full $75,000, but do you want to borrow this much? The answer is probably yes. By borrowing $75,000 you will be earning not only 13% per year on your investment of $25,000 but also an extra 1% (13% return - 12% interest cost) per year on the borrowed $75,000. This extra 1% on $75,000 means you are earning an additional 3% on your $25,000 investment (1% x $75,000 = $750, $750 ÷ $25,000 = 3%). So your total return on your investment is not 13% but 16%. If you could borrow more in this case, the return on your cash investment would be even higher. This is called leveraging and this is why many real estate investors like to maximize their borrowings when purchasing property.

However, one of the problems with maximizing your borrowings is that you may not have the ability to carry the property if unexpected costs arise. As well, if your property does not end up returning as much as you thought on a pre-interest and pre-tax basis, you could end up losing money.

Leveraging

Leveraging is using other people's money to increase the return on your own invested capital.

Let's say that you have an opportunity to purchase a $100,000 property which you expect to be able to sell in one year for $130,000. This is an increase in the value of the property of 30%. Let's say you have one of two choices to make — you can raise $100,000 of your own cash to buy the property outright, or you can invest $20,000 of your own funds and borrow the balance of $80,000 at 11%.

If you raised the $100,000 in personal funds and bought the property, your return on your investment when you sold the property one year later would be 30% ($30,000 profit ÷ $100,000 investment).

If, on the other hand, you had paid only $20,000 down and

borrowed the balance at 11%, your return on your investment when you sold the property one year later would be approximately 106% ($30,000 profit - $8,800 interest cost) ÷ $20,000 investment). This is the power of leveraging. You have used borrowed money to generate an extra return on your invested capital. Of course, this example is oversimplified to demonstrate how leveraging works. Leveraging will give you a greater overall return when the rate of return on the investment, without borrowing, is greater than the cost of borrowing.

However, there is a risk that the property's value will not increase fast enough to cover the extra interest costs associated with the borrowed funds. Using the above example, let's say the property's value increased by only $5,000 in one year rather than $30,000. The rate of return in this case, using borrowed funds, would be negative 19% ($5,000 profit - $8,800 interest cost) ÷ $20,000 investment). In other words you would have lost money through leveraging instead of making a profit of $5,000 if you had used only your own money to buy the property.

For most investors starting out in real estate, whether or not to leverage an investment is not an issue because few people have the cash available to pay for the cost of a property without borrowing. Therefore, most investors reap the benefits and suffer the risks of leveraging by default. The real danger is that the average investor will overleverage or borrow too much to buy a property. If the amount of debt used to buy property is too high relative to the investor's equity, the investor could be in the unfortunate position of not being able to carry the property. When the property is non-income-producing, such as vacant land, and the costs are relatively fixed, a downturn in the investor's personal financial position could force a sale of the property before it had increased enough to offset the costs of borrowing. If the property is income-producing, anything could happen. Rental income could go down because of increased vacancies. Costs could go up because of unexpected repairs and maintenance. The investor's personal financial situation could deteriorate.

If an investor is stretched to the limit in terms of cash flow just to make the purchase, any unexpected problems could force a sale at a loss. Therefore, the general rule of thumb should be to borrow only as much as is safely possible. "Safely possible " means borrowing at a rate which is less than the expected rate of return on the investment before borrowing costs are counted, and keeping total interest costs low enough so that you will have enough income either from the property or other sources to cover extraordinary expenses.

Timing

Timing is very important in real estate investing. It may not seem like it, but real estate prices do move down as well as up. Simply purchasing property at any time without regard to certain cyclical factors which influence real estate prices is a recipe for failure.

Timing factors which affect the price of real estate include the following:

General Business Cycles. While our economy seems to be expanding in the long run, it does suffer periods of recession and accelerating economic growth. This general business cycle is bound to affect the price of real estate. During a recession businesses fail, jobs are lost, people move, commercial tenants go bankrupt, others reorganize and consolidate. As a result, commercial space becomes available with fewer takers. People move in search of new jobs or can no longer afford the house they have. Houses are put on the resale market. People who would otherwise have purchased these properties defer purchases until the economy turns around. Real estate prices are depressed.

As the economy comes out of a recession the demand for commercial space and homes increases, inflationary forces take hold, and the prices of these commodities increase. While you cannot predict when an economy will turn around, a general awareness of these cycles should make you cautious in purchasing property after the economy has experienced a long period of growth. Similarly, you should be ready to look for opportunities to buy after the economy has been in recession for a long period of time.

Local Business Economics. Local business economies may move in a different cycle from the general economy if there are special factors affecting the economy. For example, in 1982 many parts of Canada started experiencing a period of economic growth. However, parts of the Western provinces did not participate in this general expansion as much as they might have, due to depressed oil prices. Factors such as this which could affect local economies must be given consideration.

Community Life Cycle. Most communities go through a life cycle which affects real estate prices in that community. A knowledge of the general life cycle will help an investor identify the stage at which a particular community is in its development, and will help to determine what to expect in the future in terms of development and real estate prices.

Most communities start as farmland. As a result of population increases, pressure builds to subdivide the farmland for residential purposes. Along with residential development comes highways, freeways, shopping centres and other commercial uses of property. A general economic boom is now underway. Property prices escalate dramatically during this period. Industrial use of property increases. Apartment buildings and low-income housing is constructed to accommodate people who do not want to or cannot purchase single family dwellings. The population density increases, congestion and pollution increases. Land and building prices are peaking and perhaps stagnating. Many homeowners are leaving the community's (now a city) centre in search of more desirable areas outside the city. A large residential resale market has developed in the city and outlying districts are experiencing a residential boom. The inner city homes are acquired by people either willing to accept inner city life or investors who turn homes into residential rental properties, commercial properties or light industrial properties. As a result of mixed incompatible use, homeowners finally leave the inner city. Neglect, vandalism and abandonment of property follows. Commercial and industrial property owners move their businesses out of the area. Real estate prices have been dropping steadily during this period. Decay has set in. Eventually someone decides that it would be worthwhile renovating a building. Rehabilitation begins and prices start to increase as the area once again becomes attractive.

This is the general life cycle of a community. It is difficult to say how long any community will remain at any stage, or even if it will move to the next stage. However, you should try to get an idea of where the community you are investigating is located in the cycle, if for no other reason than to satisfy yourself that it is not entering a period of decline.

Sources of Financing

The main sources of financing for the new investor are commercial banks, trust companies and mortgage companies. Each of these sources has their own requirements regarding the types of property they can or prefer to mortgage, the terms of repayment, and the interest rate charged. In addition, they have restrictions on the percentage of the purchase price they will lend on a first mortgage. This percentage could be from something very low to as high as 75% to 80%, depending on the property.

Loans on second mortgages from these same institutions are also available, but at higher rates of interest and on different terms of repayment than on a first mortgage. The total amount of borrowings possible by giving a first and second mortgage to these institutions on a property seldom exceeds 85%.

In addition to these more traditional sources of funds, there are many private investors who provide loans on first, second and sometimes even third mortgages. Of course the interest rates on these loans will usually be higher than that charged by the more traditional sources.

For large real estate investments, the primary sources of financing in Canada are life insurance companies and pension funds.

Tax Issues

There are several income tax rules which are specifically related to real estate investments. These include:

Capital Gains Vs. Income. Whenever property is sold for a profit, many investors assume that the profit will be treated as a capital gain for income tax purposes and taxed at a lower rate than other types of income. However, Revenue Canada, believes with support from the courts, that depending on the facts, a profit on the sale of property may be considered as regular income which is taxed at regular tax rates.

The facts required to arrive at this result usually involve situations where a person has bought a piece of vacant or raw land with the intention of reselling it for a profit at the first opportunity. In these situations the land is treated as if it was just like any other inventory item that a person bought and sold. Revenue Canada could also apply its "income" argument to situations where a person bought a rental property with the intention of selling it for a profit as soon as possible.

If you are planning to get involved in either of the above two types of situations you should carefully consider how successful Revenue Canada would be in applying their "income" argument if they reviewed your case. Otherwise you could find yourself in a difficult position if you had counted on a certain amount of after-tax cash from the sale of one property as the down payment on the purchase of another, only to discover that you owed twice as much tax on that sale as you had originally planned.

Capital Cost Allowance. Capital cost allowance is a notional expense which is deducted from rental revenues when calculating income for tax purposes. It is the tax equivalent to accounting depreciation. Like depreciation, capital cost allowance is calculated as a percentage of the cost of a building, furniture and/or equipment used to earn the rental income. Capital cost allowance cannot be claimed on land. That includes both vacant land and land which is sitting underneath a building.

There are several rules relating to the deduction of capital cost allowance. One of the more important ones is that capital cost allowance may not be claimed as an expense to the extent that it produces a loss for tax purposes or increases a loss that already exists. As an example, let's say you have a simple income statement that looks like this:

Rental revenue	$10,000
Operating expenses	(6,000)
Miscellaneous expenses	(500)
Interest costs	(2,500)
Net income before capital cost allowance	$ 1,000

Assume that $3,000 of capital cost allowance is available as a deduction. In this example, only $1,000 of this capital cost allowance could be claimed as an expense, i.e., just enough to reduce the project's net income to nil. If the project had recorded a loss before claiming any capital cost allowance then no capital cost allowance could be claimed.

The purpose of this rule is to prevent investors from producing tax losses based on capital cost allowance claims which could then be deducted from other types of income such as employment income or business income.

Soft Costs. Income tax rules require that certain expenses attributable to the period of construction, renovation, or alteration of a building, or in respect of the ownership of the related land during that period, must be added to the capital cost of the property rather than deducted as a current expense. These expenses are known as "soft costs" and include among other things interest, legal and accounting fees, insurance and property taxes.

If you are renovating a building you should review with your tax advisor all of the costs you incur during the period of renovation to determine which can be claimed as an expense and which cannot.

Carrying Costs. If you are holding vacant land for investment purposes, certain tax rules may restrict the deduction of property taxes on the land and interest on borrowed money used to buy the land. Rather than treating these costs as current expenses, tax law requires that they be added to the original cost of the property. As a result, when the property is sold, the cost for tax purposes is higher than it otherwise would be and the gain is lower.

These are just some of the tax rules related to real estate investing. Tax law is usually very complex and changes frequently. For these reasons you should consult your professional tax advisor to determine how the rules apply to your particular circumstances.

GOING IT ALONE OR WITH OTHERS

Should you invest by yourself or should you get involved with a group of other people? Some very successful real estate investors got their start by forming a group to buy their first property. If you do not have the financial resources to invest in an attractive piece of real estate by yourself, a smaller piece of the deal can sometimes be better than no piece at all.

Investing in groups is not for everyone. In fact, the more likely trend of your investment future will be for you to invest by yourself wherever possible and, on occasion, for one reason or another to get involved with a group. Some people start off in a group simply because it is more comforting to enter a new venture with some support. If the group has diversified skills, such as legal, accounting, real estate management or maintenance, there could be a division of labour which could help the first-time investor.

If you are considering putting together or joining a group, you should try to find a group that is as compatible as possible. When selecting the group, you would look for similarities in as many of the following categories as possible:

Objectives. The objectives of each individual and the group as a whole should be identical. It will not do the group any good to discover after a property has been purchased that some members were looking to make a profit on a quick flip while others were looking for a long-term investment from which rents were to be the major source of return.

Financial Position. The financial positions of each member of the group should be similar. Costs for maintenance and repair which are insignificant to one person could mean a great deal to someone else who is less financially secure. Agreement on any financial matters would be extremely difficult to achieve when the disparities in wealth are too great.

Age. When it comes to understanding life in general there is a generation gap, and it does not take too many years of difference to make that gap evident. On average, people who grew up in the fifties have a different outlook than those who grew up in the thirties or forties. It's only natural that this should be the case since each group grew up in a different world. In many areas of our lives the differences do not matter. However, when we have to work together as peers in an investment, these differences could become a major source of friction.

Personalities. Try to find a group that gets along. This probably means restricting the group to people who know each other and have worked or played together in the past. Personality clashes are the fastest way to get the investment group off on the wrong foot.

Once your group has been assembled, you should consider the following factors:

Get The Money Up Front. As a group, agree on your objectives, agree on the approximate investments of each person, then get the money! Put the money in a bank account and then go out and look for the property. If you do not take these steps, there is a good chance you will lose whatever investment opportunity you find because it will take too much time to raise the money and you will not be able to commit to the purchase until you have secured the financing. Raising the money first is also a test of how serious a potential group member is when asked to invest. Many people will say yes, they are interested, but when the time comes to put up their cash it is another story. With the money in the bank, you know that there is a commitment and that the group member has the financial capability to honour that commitment. The entire cost of an investment would not be required — just the group member's share of the estimated equity requirement after financing the type of property you are seeking.

Percentage Of Investment. Each investor's share in an investment should be approximately the same to avoid potential conflicts. Someone with a 60% share in an investment, for example, is going to feel that he or she has a greater say in what to do with the investment than someone with a 5% share.

Forms of Group Investing

There are several legal forms that group investing can take, including general and limited partnerships, joint ventures and corporations. There is nothing magical about any one form since they all basically recognize that each member of the group has an interest in the group investment and that each member has certain rights and obligations associated with that interest. However, there are some differences worth mentioning.

Partnerships. A partnership is a legal agreement between two or more persons for the purpose of carrying on business for a profit. The legal document specifically details the rights and obligations of the partners, e.g., the amount of the investment each must make, the sharing of expenses, and the allocation of profit and loss to each partner. It can be used for a single investment or for a continuing business relationship.

There are two types of partnership — general and limited. Under a general partnership, each partner is liable for the debts of the partnership. Income is computed at the partnership level and allocated out to each partner according to the terms of the partnership agreement. While general partnerships have their uses, they are not the most popular form for group investing simply because of the unlimited liability and the difficulty of selling a general partnership interest.

A more popular type of partnership for group investing is the limited partnership. All the rights and obligations of the partners are defined in a limited partnership agreement. The liability of each partner is limited to his or her investment. The units of a limited partnership are similar in nature to shares of a corporation. They usually have a fixed cost. Each partner buys enough units at this cost to equal his or her investment. The units are more easily disposed of than interests in a general partnership. If, for example, a partner has 100 units of a limited partnership, he or she could sell any portion of this number to other group members or to an outsider without as much trouble as in selling a general partnership interest.

Public Real Estate Syndications. You may not want the bother or trouble of putting your own group together. You would rather leave the investing to the professionals and invest in whatever opportunities they find, in much the same way you would invest in a mutual fund of stocks. You want a return at the end of the year that is hassle free.

It is possible to invest this way in real estate through a public real estate syndication. The most common method of organizing such a syndication is through a public offering of units in a limited partnership put together for a specific project. This project could be anything from the purchase and rental of stores and restaurant franchises to construction and operation of major hotels. The main advantage of such a deal is that it is clean. You do not have to look for property, maintain it, find tenants, manage it, sell it, and so on. A few disadvantages are that you have little or no control over what the partnership is doing, you usually do not know the organizers or the other unitholders, and your return may be lower than if you invested on your own.

Before investing in a public real estate syndication you should analyze the property or project carefully to see if it is a worthwhile investment. You should also have a clear picture of who the organizers are, their history in other deals, and their ability to do the job required. Finally, you should study the partnership agreement very carefully, preferably with an expert, to determine what your rights and obligations are. For example, can the partnership call on you for more money if the project costs more than anticipated, can you drop out of the investment with little or no financial or legal hardship, etc.

Joint Ventures. A joint venture is similar in nature to a partnership. However, it is less formal and more temporary. Joint ventures are usually formed by investors for a large project to which each investor brings his or her own skills, money or other assets. If a joint venture arrangement is desired, care must be taken to ensure that it is not considered a partnership since different tax and legal consequences will result.

Corporations. A corporation is a separate legal entity. Shares or debt instruments are issued to various investors and the funds are used to purchase whatever investment the group wishes. There are some advantages to using a corporation, the chief one being that liability is limited to the amount invested in the corporation by the shareholder/creditor. However, corporations are generally not popular as a method of group investing partly because of the costs associated with organizing a corporation and filing separate tax returns. As well, income is calculated and taxed in the corporation and can only be distributed to investors in the form of salaries or dividends. Generally, the desire for limited liability associated with corporations can be satisfied by a limited partnership.

SPECIFIC TYPES OF REAL ESTATE OPPORTUNITIES

Raw Land. The purchase of raw land with the intention of developing it or reselling it for a profit is probably the most speculative of the various types of real estate purchases. This type of property is usually left to the experienced professional who is well aware of all the problems and risks that go hand-in-hand with raw land. For example, you never know when, or even if, the expansion of the community you were anticipating will reach the property you are holding. If it does reach you, you do not know what kinds of zoning or environment restrictions will affect your land. The expansion plans for a city may include designating your land as green space which the city is willing to expropriate at a price near your cost or even below your cost.

During the period between your purchase and the eventual resale, the raw land will be earning no income. You will have to cover all carrying costs such as property taxes and interest costs yourself. Financing from banks and other lending institutions is difficult to obtain because of the speculative nature of raw land and its lack of income to service the debt. As a result there is very little leverage possible on such deals. In addition, profits from the sale of raw land are generally not considered to be capital gains for tax purposes. Consequently, these profits are taxed at the same rates as regular income.

The best way for someone without a lot of experience to invest in raw land is to purchase a piece of land that is attractive to the purchaser for whatever reason, and pay cash or a large down payment. For example, the property could be a nice lot in cottage country. The purchase should be made with the understanding that it is a long-term investment that may or may not be profitable in the future.

Single Family Dwellings. Single family houses are one of the more attractive investments the beginning investor can make. Most investors are familiar with houses since they have already bought one to live in. Tenants are usually stable. There are plenty of homes to choose from at any one time. Financing is normally easy to obtain. There is a minimum of management time and effort. The price is normally low compared to other types of real estate.

However, there are some disadvantages to single family homes as an investment. The market can be volatile and even speculative on occasion. The costs of tenant vacancy is quite high since only one tenant's rent is covering all the expenses. Maintenance costs are usually higher for a rental home than for an owner-occupied home. Yearly cash flow yields are usually low. In other words most of your profit will have to come from the sale of the property rather than from yearly income. And while there is an opportunity to make a profit investing in single family homes, there is seldom the opportunity to make a large profit.

Apartments. Apartments come in all shapes and sizes, from duplexes which have only two units either side-by-side or on top of each other to triplexes, to medium-sized buildings with six to ten units to the largest buildings with 100 to 150 or more units.

Apartments can be a good real estate investment as long as you do not buy more than you can handle, either from a financial point of view or a management and experience point of view. The opportunity for profit is often good, the risk factors are moderate to low, leverage can be quite high, and there is usually a good resale market.

Cash flows from apartments which are medium-sized or greater are relatively stable and are not especially sensitive to tenant vacancies. However, they can be quite low, especially if rents are subject to rent control legislation. Cash flows from duplexes, triplexes and fourplexes are more sensitive to tenant vacancies than larger buildings. If one or two units in these smaller buildings are vacant for any period of time the owner is going to be required to cover a relatively large portion of the costs of the building.

An advantage to apartment buildings is that rents and therefore profits are often responsive to upgrades and renovations. Many investors have made good profits buying an apartment building at a price based on its expected return as it is currently maintained, upgrading the building, increasing the rents, and selling the property to another investor at a price based on the new rents.

However, apartments take work and experience. Tenants are always coming and going, and continual maintenance is required.

The natural progression for an investor is to start with a single family dwelling, a duplex or even a triplex before moving on to larger apartment buildings. In any case the costs of large apartments together with the financial resources required to weather unexpected problems usually mean that the small investor will be unable to consider large apartment buildings except as part of a group.

Condominiums. Investing in a condominium can be a good choice if it looks like the condominium is in a location where demand will cause it to appreciate in value. The best locations for condominiums for appreciation are in downtown areas where demand is high, and in popular vacation sites. Condominiums have their advantages and disadvantages. They often cost less than houses, therefore the initial investment is usually smaller for the new investor. Rents are usually higher than apartment units, although tenants are often easier to find because units are usually larger and more private than apartments. Condominium units usually require less maintenance than a house, however, maintenance fees for common area maintenance expenses such as repairs to an underground garage could be quite high. The condominium market is extremely difficult to predict. A good building in a good location could be very attractive one year, and three years later developers could have constructed more condominium buildings in the immediate vicinity keeping prices stable or even driving prices down.

Retail Stores. Investment in retail property can include anything from a single retail store on a neighbourhood corner, to a store in a strip mall, to an entire shopping centre. While single stores and even small strip malls are owned by investors with no particular expertise in the area, the larger shopping centres are usually undertaken by experienced individuals or groups which have the financial resources and expertise to deal with the complex legal, accounting and management problems associated with such large commercial undertakings.

For the new investor, starting small is still the best advice. Experience with commercial leases, and business in general, must be gained in order to be successful at investing in retail stores. From a business point of view you should be able to assess whether your tenant will be a success or not. If the business succeeds you will also succeed, provided your lease allows you to earn an acceptable rate of return. If you ignore the tenant's chances of success you could find yourself with a succession of business failures, broken leases, bad debts and court cases.

Office Buildings. Investing in office buildings is similar to investing in retail stores. They can be profitable if you know what you are doing. They can range in size from small buildings with one or two tenants to skyscrapers. It is unlikely that a new investor will have either the capital or experience to invest in anything but a small building unless it is done with a group. Once again the quality of the tenant and the terms of the lease are very important. Location, convenience, address, appearance, etc., are all important factors to consider in being able to attract good tenants.

Other Investments. In addition to the types of real estate investments outlined above there are several other types available including industrial real estate, land development, and tax shelters. These and other similar types of investments would normally only be considered by a new investor on the advice or in consultation with professional advisors in that area.

CHAPTER 5

MUTUAL FUNDS
By Bill McLeod

INTRODUCTION

Mutual funds are one of Canada's fastest-growing investment media. Thousands of people own them or are considering buying them. In this section of *Guide to Making Money* I'll try to explain the basic concepts of the funds and spell out some consumer guidelines for purchasing them.

Essentially, mutual funds are glorified investment clubs. People pool their savings which are then invested on their behalf. When you invest in a mutual fund you buy shares which, in turn, represent tiny, pro-rated portions of whatever the funds invest in. These tiny portions are calculated to the third decimal point.

Mutual funds invest in many things. Common stocks, bonds, mortgages and real estate are the most common types of mutual fund investments. The funds that invest in common stocks are the most glamorous, the most publicized and the most risky.

There are several different reasons for the popularity of mutual fund investing. Baby boomers have rapidly increasing pools of cash with which to invest. The funds are heavily promoted, particularly around RRSP time. Stock markets have enjoyed an unprecedented boom well into the last half of the decade. In recent years, interest rates have declined dramatically, causing investors to look for a better return on their money. And, finally, with the removal of tax on capital gains for most Canadians, investing in the stock market has become very attractive.

INVESTING IN MUTUAL FUNDS

The advantages of investing in mutual funds far outweigh the disadvantages. I'll list and briefly explain both. The list or ranking is not in any particular order. And since most investment in mutual funds is in common stock or equity-based funds, this segment will apply only to those types of funds.

Advantages

Diversification. Probably the most attractive feature of the funds is the fact that an investment as small as $20.00 can be spread over or into the shares of hundreds of corporations.

Convenience. You can buy mutual funds as easily as falling off the proverbial log. They can be purchased at banks, trust companies, life insurance companies, from mutual fund sales people and directly from the funds themselves.

Regularity of Investing. In most cases, you can invest a small regular amount of money in the fund of your choice, using an automatic deduction from your bank account.

Liquidity. Another attractive feature of investing in mutual funds is that you can cash in almost whenever you wish. Most funds are valued on a daily basis, and you can get your money out any business day.

Information. Since the unit or share values of most funds are listed in most daily newspapers, you can easily monitor how well your fund or funds are doing. In addition, the *Financial Times* publishes a comprehensive monthly analysis of all funds and an excellent *Sourcebook*. The *Financial Post* publishes a quarterly feature on the funds that is quite good, but not as detailed as the one put out by the *Financial Times*.

Cost. The cost of investing in mutual funds is very low. Usually it is less than 2% per year of the amount invested. The cost is deducted from the investment income that the fund receives, and what is left is passed on to the fund's shareholders in the form of new or additional shares. Compared to the cost of buying shares in individual companies, the 2% is a pittance. (This 2% is not to be confused with acquisition or sales charges which will be described in detail later.)

Professional Management. This a more complicated and less straightforward advantage than the rest. It is true that mutual funds are managed by professionals. They get paid for what they do, but some of them don't do it very well. In any given time period, most mutual fund managers do worse than chance. But the good ones are very good. Many have achieved rates of return averaging around 20% per year over many years.

International Investing. Canadians who would like to invest in the U.S., Japanese or European markets can do so easily by purchasing one or more funds available in Canada that invest in markets outside the country.

Disadvantages

Risk. Investing in the stock market directly carried with it an inherent risk. Doing it through a mutual fund reduced that risk but does not eliminate it. The investment is not insured by the Canada Deposit Insurance Corporation. In addition, most funds do badly when the stock market does badly. Drops of 20% in the value of the funds' shares are not uncommon; they occur every four or five years. But since mutual funds are long-term investments, these drops should be anticipated and ignored.

Unscrupulous Sales People and Sales Practices. Because mutual fund investing has become so popular, the field has attracted its fair share of charlatans.

Management Fees and Sales Charges

There are two kinds of charges for investing in mutual funds. The first is a management fee as described earlier. It is collected by all mutual funds, usually by deduction from the investment income earned by the fund. It varies from 1 to 2% of the value of the fund. It is used to pay the normal business costs of running the fund — investment management fees, brokerage, auditors' fees, office expenses, advertising, etc. The size of the fee varies according to how the fund chooses to do business and the size of the fund. If the fund chooses to do a lot of expensive promotion, other things being equal, the management fee will be higher.

Generally, the larger the fund, the smaller the management fee, becaused fixed expenses are spread over a greater number of shares and shareholders. The management fee is best illustrated by the term "expense ratio", which must be shown in the fund's prospectus. The fee itself is not an important factor in the choice of a fund and it is accounted for in the performance figures quoted in the *Financial Times'* monthly report on the funds.

The Front-End Load

Unlike management fees, front-end loading charges are associated only with funds sold by salespeople or stockbrokers. The charge varies between 1% and 9% of the amount of money invested. It is a one shot, non-repeating levy.

In most cases, the load is negotiable. Of course, many salespeople try to get the 9%. In major urban centers where competition is keen, 5% is the rule. In outlying areas the full 9% is not uncommon.

Contrary to what many mutual fund salespeople will tell you, there is no relationship whatsoever between sales charges and investment performance.

There are several good no-load funds available and they will be identified in the "tips" section that will close out this chapter.

Hidden Loads and Rear-End Loads

As consumers have become more sophisticated and have forced down front-end loads, at least one fund has hidden its front-end load in the management fee. That, by itself, is not all that bad. But it has presented itself to the public as a no-load fund.

In addition, that same fund has a sliding withdrawal charge. It starts at 4% and goes down to nothing if the fund is held long enough. Withdrawal charges or back-end loads are quite uncommon and should be avoided.

MUTUAL FUNDS AND YOUR RRSP

Particularly in February, great pressure is exerted by some funds on the consuming public to buy mutual fund-based RRSPs. The advantage is that, historically, the funds have performed much better than fixed income-based investments. However, what is not widely discussed is the fact that, once placed inside an RRSP, mutual funds lose the preferential treatment accorded to both dividends and capital gains. The accumulated value of the RRSP will eventually be taxed as if it had been interest.

Most independent advisors recommend that their clients do their mutual fund investing outside their RRSP and their fixed income investing inside the tax shelter. This strategy will become even more important if and when the $1,000 investment income deduction is abolished.

An exception to the rule about keeping mutual funds outside the RRSP is the case of a young person who has no interest income and who wishes to take advantage of the higher return generally associated with equity-based investments.

GETTING OUT OF YOUR RRSP "TAX FREE"

A very alarming development in the personal finance field began to take place early in 1986. Seminars were being advertised in the national press that purported to show people how to get out of their RRSPs "Tax Free".

Here is how the scam worked. Consumers were advised to borrow an amount of money about 10 times what they wanted to take out of their RRSP. They were then advised to use the borrowed money to buy mutual funds and to take an amount out of the RRSP equal to the interest they would have to pay on the loan. Since the loan interest was tax deductible, it would offset the amount withdrawn from the RRSP, which was taxable. If the mutual fund growth exceeded the interest payable on the loan that would be a bonus.

However, no mention was made of the possibility that interest rates could go up and fund performance could go down. Both can and have happened. If these two events occurred simultaneously, people who used this strategy would be in very serious trouble.

Neither was any mention made of the expenses that would be incurred if the loan had to be secured by a mortgage on a personal residence as it often had to be. Expenses include mortgage insurance, legal fees and survey costs. Nor was any mention made of the front-end load that had to be paid on the funds that were being recommended.

The bottom line of course is that the scheme was very questionable at best and, at worst, downright bad advice.

If the deductibility of interest on investment loans disappears with tax reform, so will this scam. But, until then, beware.

LEVERAGING

Another version of the Getting Out of Your RRSP "Tax Free" scheme was just straight leveraging. Mutual fund sales people were persuading consumers to borrow huge amounts of money to buy mutual funds. One person I know went for the scheme to the tune of $300,000, secured by a mortgage on the family farm.

Again, as long as fund performance exceeded the rate of interest payable on the loan, the scheme worked. But once interest rates exceeded fund performance, the borrower could be in very serious trouble.

Tough questions should be asked of any lending institution that provides funds for such a scam. Obviously, those questions are not being asked.

SAVING FOR A CHILD'S EDUCATION

There are four common strategies for saving for a child's education: putting the money in a bank account, buying a life insurance policy, buying a Registered Education Savings Plan, or buying a couple of mutual funds.

Bank Account. If you put the money in a bank account, a low rate of return could be anticipated. With the apparent demise of the $1,000 investment income deduction and the switch from deductions to credits, putting money in a bank account could very well have some unpleasant down-the-road tax implications.

Life Insurance. Buying a life insurance policy that mixes savings and investments is a dumb thing to do at any time. But buying such a combination for a child is especially unwise. The rate of return on the savings portion is negative for many years, low in the long term, not disclosed, and impossible to calculate. Price comparison among companies that sell similar products is difficult, if not impossible. If the child should die, the life insurance company simply keeps the savings portion (the cash surrender value). And when the child needs the money to go to university or college, the life insurance company may very well resist letting it go. They have a history of trying to persuade young people to leave the money with the company in another type of low-quality life insurance policy.

Registered Education Savings Plans. RESPs, such as those sold by the Canadian Scholarship Trust and University Scholarships of Canada, also have their drawbacks. Suppose the child receives the maximum of three scholarships after having received the return of payments at age 18. At present the scholarship levels are approximately $1,500 each. The average rate of return on the whole scheme will be about 9% to 11% below what the good mutual funds are paying.

If the child does not attend a qualifying post-secondary institution, all of the interest on all of the money paid into the plan is lost.

All of the scholarship money will be taxable in the child's hands. What that will mean after tax reform is anybody's guess.

And finally, these plans discriminate against the child who chooses to attend a community college where programs are normally of two and three years' duration. For a two-year program, only one, not three scholarships would be paid out. It would be two for a three-year program. This same disadvantage would apply to the three year Pass B.A. Programs at Ontario Universities.

Mutual Fund. Perhaps the best way for a parent or grandparent to put money away for a child's education is to make a monthly investment in a mutual fund. Many funds will accept contributions as low as $15.00 a month in the form of an automatic withdrawal from a bank account.

The advantage of this strategy is compelling. There is no tax on the investment income earned in the form of capital gain until the fund is cashed in. If the gain does not exceed the proposed lifetime exemption of $100,000, no tax will ever be paid. The dividends earned by the funds are very small and, for most people, are insignifcant.

Unlike the Registered Education Savings Plans mentioned earlier, the funds remain the property of the investor. They can be used for any educational institution. Or if the child decides not to go to college, they can be given to the child, kept by the parent or transferred to another child.

BOND, MORTGAGE AND INCOME FUNDS

Many consumers are buying mutual funds that invest in bonds, mortgages and other fixed income types of vehicles. This may not be a very good idea. The values of these funds drop dramatically as interest rates rise, and rise dramatically as interest rates fall. As interest rates have dropped drastically in recent months, some of these funds have had spectacular short-term performance figures. Fund salespeople have been implying that this performance is a result of good management and can be expected to repeat itself. Nothing could be further from the truth. All that the performance figures on income-based mutual funds can tell us is where interest rates have been. And we already know that.

DIVIDEND FUNDS

Another type of mutual fund that seems to be increasing in popularity is the dividend fund. It is really an equity-based fund that selects stocks that pay high dividends rather than those with high growth potential. People who buy shares in these funds hope that the tax break they get on dividends offsets the generally low yield. This theoretical advantage will be less attractive if tax reform reduces the preferential treatment accorded to dividends.

Dividend funds are very poor RRSP choices because they have low growth and low yield, both of which are treated eventually as interest when the RRSP is terminated.

UNSCRUPULOUS SALES PRACTICES

Over the years a number of unscrupulous mutual fund sales practices have been brought to my attention. Among them are the following:

- There can be a conflict of interest. Some fund salespeople have been holding themselves out as financial planners and consultants of one sort or another. You can sell mutual funds. Or you can sell information and advice. But you can't do both.
- Fund performance figures are quoted that do not identify or include sales commissions.
- Performance figures are quoted for unreasonable time periods such as one year.
- Management fees are not adequately explained.
- Failure to advise consumers of the risks inherent in investing in equity-based funds occurs.
- The abuse of recent performance figures for bond and mortgage-based funds was outlined earlier.
- Consumers are advised to place equity-based funds inside the RRSP tax shelter when the funds should be kept outside the RRSP.

- Consumers are influenced to borrow huge amounts of money to buy mutual funds.
- It is implied that front-end loaded funds perform better than no-load funds.
- Senior citizens are pressured to buy mutual fund-based Registered Retirement Income Funds when interest-based vehicles could be more appropriate.
- Funds are churned. One fund is recommended to replace another one on a regular basis. The only purpose for doing this may be to generate another sales commission.
- It is implied that a fund has no front-end load when, in fact, the load is hidden in the management fee.
- Funds are sold that have hidden sales rewards and prizes, and are not necessarily the best funds for their customers.

NINE TIPS ON BUYING MUTUAL FUNDS

1. Inform yourself. Buy or read the *Financial Times* and the *Financial Post* regularly, particularly the *Times*. Buy the *Financial Times Sourcebook* if you are at all serious.
2. Use the funds for the purpose for which they are intended — to provide small investors with a chance to get into the stock market at minimum risk and, at the same time, take advantage of the preferential tax treatment accorded to dividends and capital gains.
3. Remember that the stock market goes up and it goes down. But in the long run the trend is up. Don't let market corrections panic you.
4. Start a monthly investment program, preferably with an automatic bank withdrawal.
5. Don't pay a front-end load unless you really have to do so.
6. If you want to buy a front-end loaded fund, buy it through a discount broker such as Marathon Brown. Their maximum sales commission is 4%.
7. Keep an eye out for slips in performance that may signify a change in management.
8. Watch for Income Tax changes that may affect the tax you pay on your investment income.
9. Two superb Canadian no-load funds are Royfund (sold at all branches of the Royal Bank) and the Canadian Anaesthetists' Mutual Fund (Suite 901, 94 Cumberland Street, Toronto, Ontario, M5R 1A3). Both are RRSP eligi-

ble. For a more complete listing of no-load funds' performance read the *Canadian MoneySaver*.

Two excellent international funds are Montreal Trust International (available at all Montreal Trust Branches) and Bolton Tremblay (available through Marathon Brown).

CHAPTER 6

LOW-RISK INVESTING

By Donald Pooley

INTRODUCTION

Want to become a millionaire fast? Then you're reading the wrong article. This is about low-risk investing — accumulating wealth safely and surely over the long term. You may make a million along the way, but that's not one of the objectives.

AVOID LOSING MONEY

Our first objective is to avoid losing money. This means sticking to low-risk investments. It also means learning to measure risk, so we know which investments to avoid.

LONG-TERM INVESTING

Our second objective is to invest for the long term. This helps us to sleep at night without worrying about which way our investments went today, or where they'll go tomorrow. All we want to know is that over the long haul they're growing at an above-average pace.

Investing for the long term also allows us to take advantage of the power of compounding. Compounding just means reinvesting your growth, which doesn't sound like a big deal. But over the long term it greatly enhances the advantages of small short-term gains. For example, how long does it take to double your money at a growth rate of 10% per year? Without compounding it takes 10 years. With compounding it takes only 7.2 years.

Now triple the time to 30 years. Without compounding your 10% annually has tripled your 10-year return. But compounding gives you more than 15 times as much as your 7.2 year gain!

Long-term investing also reduces the amount you'll pay in brokerage commissions. Brokers make a commission every time you buy or sell something. This is true regardless of whether you're investing in houses, the stock market, or just about anything else. If you do a lot of buying and selling in a given period, more of your money will go to brokers (and less to your investments) than if you don't. The low-risk investor looks for good investments he can stay with for a long time, and pays less of his money to brokers.

Many people think of low-risk investments as bank accounts, term deposits, Canada Savings Bonds, and other things that pay interest and guarantee your capital. These are better thought of as "no-risk" investments. You're unlikely to lose the dollars you invest in them, providing you don't have too many in one institution.

Diversify

By dividing your savings among different financial institutions you diversify your investments. You've learned not to put "all your eggs in one basket". Diversifying like this reduces the risk to you of a bank failing without enough deposit insurance to cover your savings.

There's another risk, though, to having all your money in interest-paying investments. Interest rates change. The high rates you could get in 1981 are not available today. Low-risk investors shield their interest-paying investments from declining interest rates by diversifying into other investments.

Some people feel that the stock market is a better place for their money to grow. They diversify by buying stocks of different industries, figuring that as one goes down the other will go up. Sometimes they're successful, and sometimes not.

Variability

Playing the stock market is not a game for the faint of heart. Even holding the top 300 stocks on the Toronto Stock Exchange is no safeguard against erratic swings. You can see this on Chart 1, which shows the performance of the TSE 300 Index over the past 10 years.

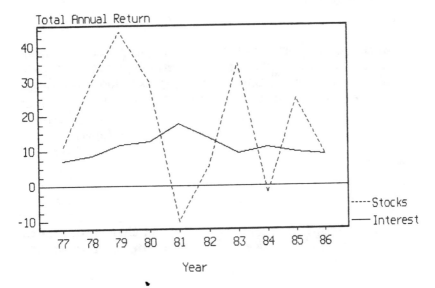

This chart also illustrates the actions of interest rates of 91-day Treasury Bills (Interest) over the past 10 years. It shows that the stock market has greater variability (wider swings) than interest rates, which means greater risk.

Chart 1 also shows that as Stocks go up Interest usually goes down, and vice versa. They're counter-cyclical. This is worth knowing because counter-cyclical investments can combine to reduce each other's variability (i.e. risk). To understand how this works we'll need to know more about measuring variability.

The wider swings of Stocks show that they have more variability than Interest. But if you're trying to compare two investments with what look like equally wide swings, how do you know which is the riskier? Fortunately there's a mathematical technique that provides a precise measurement of variability. It's called Standard Deviation. It takes the variations of an investment's annual return over a number of years and boils them down to one figure. From now on we'll call that figure risk, and use it to compare investments.

Risk

Risk is measured over time. We can't access the future so we use the past. The total annual returns of each investment over the past 5 and 10 years (ending December 31, 1986) are the sources of our risk measurements.

Reward

Reward is also measured over time. For our purposes it's the average annual compound rate of return over the same two periods. This may become clearer if we look at these measurements for the investments discussed so far.

	Risk		Reward	
	5yrs.	10yrs.	5yrs.	10yrs.
Interest (Canadian 91-day T-Bills)	1.9	3.0	10.5%	11.0%
Stocks (TSE 300 Index)	15.1	17.6	13.6%	16.3%

This table shows that risk and reward can change with time. We can use this to judge the stability of an investment.

	Risk		Reward	
	5yrs.	10yrs.	5yrs.	10yrs.
New Investment	1.5	2.6	10.8%	11.6%

New Investment has much less risk than Stocks, and even appears to have less risk than Interest. Let's see how they all look together on Chart 2.

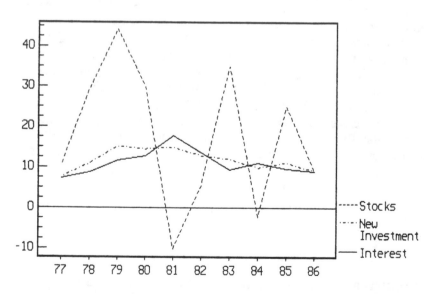

The chart confirms our risk figures. New Investment has smaller swings than Interest, less variability, and therefore less risk. Where did we find an investment with less risk than Interest?

We didn't find it, we made it. New Investment is a mix of Interest and Stocks — 90% Interest and 10% Stocks.

New Investment shows how proper diversification can reduce risk and even improve reward, especially if you can match up counter-cyclical investments.

MUTUAL FUND PORTFOLIOS

I use the same technique to reduce the risk of the mutual fund portfolios of my clients. Calculations are made of how the total portfolio would have performed every year if all the funds in it had been held in their present proportion for the last 10 years. Then the 5- and 10-year risk and reward figures are determined for the total portfolio.

Next it's necessary to find the mutual funds that can improve the present portfolio, and calculate their amounts. This requires testing a number of different combinations until the most suitable balance of 5- and 10-year risk and reward is found.

The 10-year performance figures of one client's portfolio had their lowest point in 1981. This told me to look for mutual funds that were positive in that year. After sifting through the available 10-year records of appropriate funds, and testing various combinations, three funds were selected. Added to this client's old portfolio, the right amount of each fund created his new portfolio.

	Risk		Reward	
	5yrs.	10yrs.	5yrs.	10yrs.
Old Portfolio	11.0	10.6	20.8%	20.1%
New Portfolio	8.6	8.7	22.7%	20.6%

New Portfolio provides significant improvements in both the 5- and 10-year risk levels, and more modest improvements in reward for both periods. This confirms the advantages of this technique.

Performance

Of course there are no guarantees that New Portfolio will be less risky, or perform better than Old Portfolio in the future.

But being based on the past performance figures of all the funds involved it has a much better chance of success.

The only indicators we have of what will happen in the future are our records of what happened in the past. We know the sun will rise tomorrow morning because our records of the past say that it always has. We expect future stock market prices to go up and down because our records say they always have in the past. We need records of the past so we know what to expect in the future. And the longer the period covered by such records the better it is for estimating future probabilities.

If an investment has no record, or the record is short, the low-risk investor avoids it. The odds are against a new venture being as successful as its enthusiasts say it should be. Whenever one is, its success is widely quoted by the promoters of other new ventures. They never quote the far greater number of new ventures that fail. New ventures are high-risk — avoid them.

New mutual funds are the same. They have a 50% chance of being below average, and a 75% chance of not performing as well as those in the top 25%.

It's not difficult to select mutual funds that have outperformed 75% of the rest in most of the last 10 years. Their records are available in various publications. And as all mutual funds are reported on the same basis it's easy to compare their past performance.

It's not so easy with other investments. They're reported on in ways that are not helpful to the long-term, low-risk investor. Stocks and bonds have only recent prices and returns quoted. No publication provides their total annual return over the past 10 years as they do for mutual funds. This makes it difficult to compare the performance of such investments with each other, and with mutual funds.

This is also another reason to choose mutual funds over direct investment in the stock market. The published records of mutual fund performance make it easier to avoid the consistent losers, and pick the winners.

ChartLists

In fact, given the long-term performance record of any mutual fund we can determine its risk and reward figures, and position it on a chart of one against the other. We can put a number of funds on the same chart, and decide which we like best according to where it is on the chart. The ChartList that follows is based on the 5-year figures of some RRSP funds.

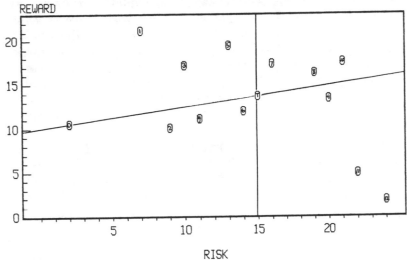

Code		Risk	Reward
0	Interest (91-day, Cdn. T-Bills)	1.9	10.5%
1	London Life Bond Fund	6.9	21.1%
2	Principal Growth Fund	9.4	10.0%
3	Guaranty Trust Mgd. RSP Equity	9.6	17.1%
4	Royal Trust Canadian Equity	10.7	11.0%
5	Industrial Growth Fund	12.6	19.4%
6	Timvest Growth Fund	14.4	11.9%
T	Stocks (TSE 300 Index)	15.1	13.6%
7	RoyFund Equity	16.3	17.3%
8	United Venture Retirement	18.8	16.2%
9	Growth Equity Fund	20.3	13.3%
10	Corporate Investors Stock Fund	20.8	17.5%
11	DK Enterprise Fund	21.2	4.8%
12	Heritage Fund	23.6	1.7%

Risk on the ChartList runs left to right (left is least). Reward runs from bottom to top (top is better). Interest and Stocks are also on it with lines running through them. The upright line through "T" separates those that are riskier than Stocks (to the right of it) from those that are less risky. The sloped line through "O" and "T" separate funds that performed better than these benchmarks (above the line) from those that didn't.

These two lines divide this chart into four areas. Funds in the upper left quadrant are preferred because they combine least risk with most reward. The closer any fund is to the upper left corner the better.

Only 12 of the over 300 mutual funds available to Canadians are on this chart. They were picked to show three in each quadrant. Most of my ChartLists have few below the sloping line. My pre-selection process eliminates most poor performers.

Subscribers to my newsletter receive ChartLists showing only the funds that pass this screening process. There are also separate ChartLists for RRSP and non-RRSP funds. If you'd like a sample copy of both, send $5 to me asking for the latest ChartLists.

My selection procedure starts with my subscription to the "Financial Post's" quarterly "Survey of Funds". Each issue ranks the funds in each section according to their average annual compound rate of return over each of 10 periods, from one to 10 years. This allows me to check those that ranked in the top 25% for each period, and then select only those that were checked for most of the 10 periods.

To test this selection technique, 25 funds were picked from the RRSP Equity Fund section of the Survey for September 30, 1985. When the one-year performance of this group was obtained from the Survey issued a year later, the average gain was 21.8%. Compare this to the 16.3% average gain of all 106 RRSP Equity Funds, and the 16.7% gain of the TSE 300 over the same period. Obviously this method produces above-average results.

After selecting funds in this way, their 5- and 10-year risk and reward figures must be calculated. This requires their total annual returns (not compounded) for each of the past 10 years. This information is not directly available from "Financial Post's" quarterly "Survey", though it can be determined from it. Fortunately the "Mutual Fund Sourcebook" published by the "Financial Times" provides the needed total annual returns without extra calculation. Also, as one publication may not cover all the funds included in the other, both are required to be sure that none are missed.

As these quarterly publications may not appear for as much as seven weeks after their cover date, weekly publications such as the "Financial Post" and the "Financial Times" are also useful. Each provides monthly fund reports, and the "Financial Times" also produces long-term performance records of most funds twice a year, usually in the third weeks of January and July. With the risk and reward figures calculated for the selected funds we can prepare their ChartLists. And with the right ChartLists you can pick the funds best suited to your situation. The monthly mutual-fund performance tables of the *Financial Post* now carries a reward/risk ratio for five years. The *Canadian MoneySaver* carries the top five performing funds for RRSP and Non-RRSP Eligible Funds. The total growth is provided for 1, 3, 5 and 10 years. Canadian, foreign and international funds are monitored. These are two more sources which could provide additional methods for selecting low-risk funds.

SUMMARY

I've tried to show you how diversification reduces risk, how to measure risk and reward, and how to use them to select low-risk investments with above-average rewards. May these concepts help you to make your wealth grow.

CHAPTER 7

INVESTING FOR GROWTH

By Nancy Foster

INTRODUCTION

When you've reached that wonderful stage of life when your income is greater than your expenditures and money is building up in your savings account you'll become increasingly uncomfortable about your money. You'll be aware that it's not working as hard for you as it could — that you could get more out of it. What do you do? Well, if you're like most Canadians you'll make a tentative call to a stockbroker asking about Treasury Bills. You may or may not actually buy one, but you have begun a learning trip about the world of investments beyond the bank (or since deregulation, increasingly, within the bank).

If you get around to opening an account with a broker, you will be asked to state your investment objectives. Trying to state your investment objectives when you don't know what is possible is difficult indeed. So what I hope to achieve in this chapter is to set out the alternatives that the stock and bond markets offer along with the kinds of return you can expect. What the broker is looking for, by the way, (and is required to ask) is your risk tolerance. What degree of risk are you prepared to accept? Now we all want the highest return with as little risk as possible. As your knowledge and assets grow your risk profile will change. You will begin to see risk in shades of grey rather than black and white. Some of the investments that you formerly thought of as free of risk (Canada Savings Bonds perhaps) you will now see as at risk from inflation and taxation. Mutual funds, which you may have ignored because of the lack of a guarantee, may be seen as solid inflation fighters.

In chapter one we examined the much-used risk pyramid — as you proceed toward the apex your potential return increases, but so does risk. Please do not assume that there is no risk near the bottom. A 6% return on a savings account can be a poor defence of your capital if taxation takes 40% and inflation 60%.

Keep your eye on real return — your gain after taxation and inflation are taken into account. You may wish to establish an interim goal of achieving, say 3% per year real return on your funds just to see where this will lead you. Again, as your assets and experience grow you may become dissatisfied with that goal.

TREASURY BILLS

My guess is that you really don't want Treasury Bills unless you are parking money. T-Bills are short-term (30 days to 364 days) government debt. They are sold at a discount. For instance, a $10,000 T-Bill yielding 8.25% to maturity would cost $9,798.50 and would mature in 91 days at $10,000. While a commission is seldom charged there is often a service charge. T-Bills can be purchased for any amount in multiples of $1,000 and unlike Guaranteed Investment Certificates can be sold prior to maturity, although you should try to tailor your maturity to your need. If, for instance, you have to pay taxes on April 30th, do not buy a T-Bill that matures on May 10.

Generally T-Bills will return a couple of points more than a savings account and will probably be slightly higher than the new T-Bill accounts offered at some trust companies.

If you have a use for your money in the forseeable future and want to raise your return while it is parked, then T-Bills are for you. If you are holding money to invest later at what you expect will be a higher rate of return, the T-Bill would be most useful. Many clients use T-Bills to hold money while their experience and ease with other financial instruments increases. Brokerage houses experience a rush into Treasury Bills in periods of declining interest rates as Guaranteed Investment Certificates mature and investors are so dissatisfied with the reinvestment rate that the money is moved to T-Bills while alternatives are explored. A similar rush is experienced when the T-Bill rate exceeds the Canada Savings Bond rate.

INCREASING YOUR INVESTMENT INCOME

Bonds

Some of you will wish to increase your disposable income and will want to deploy your capital so that the income is as high as is consistent with preservation of that capital. If so, your attention will be drawn to Government and Corporate Bonds. The rate of return on long-term Government bonds will be about 1.5% above the 91-day T-Bill rate. A top-rated Corporate bond will pay an extra 1% yield. As with all investments, yield is related to risk, with Government bonds paying the least. Under normal circumstances yield will increase as the length to maturity increases. Yield relationships vary with economic conditions. Bonds pay interest semi-annually. While a bond and a debenture are different in the type of security that is offered, the terms are increasingly used interchangeably.

New money is raised and old debt refinanced by the federal and provincial governments with distressing regularity. These new issues will have an interest rate that is set in the context of the market. Influencing the interest rate will be the safety of the issue and the prevailing interest rates at the time of issue. After issue you may sell your bond (or buy more) on the secondary market in which a typical bond quote would look like this:

CDA 11.750 01FEB03 114.00 9.959 114.25 9.93

This Government of Canada issue which was issued with an interest rate (coupon rate) of 11.75% is now selling at bid $114.00 asked $114.25, which would give a yield to the new buyer of between 9.93% and 9.959%. As you can see, this bond has responded to lower interest rates by increasing in capital value. This same bond would have been selling for less than $100.00 if interest rates had gone up above 11.75%.

Whether you buy a bond at new issue or on the secondary market will depend on whether you find the interest rate satisfactory. While you can sell your bonds if you wish, the secondary market is not very satisfying for holders of less than $25,000 in bonds. The price you receive will be well below the quotes in the newspaper. This is because your bond is purchased by the brokerage company and will have to be resold. This is very difficult to do on small amounts of obscure issues. If the yield and security of bonds interests you, you will want to

discover bond funds. For the small investor these offer professional management with easy entry and sale in small and large
amounts. Ask about mortgage funds while you're there. These
mutual funds are available through banks, trusts, brokerages
and mutual fund companies.

Mortgage-Backed Securities

New to the Canadian scene but old hat south of the border,
the mortgage-backed security may be an ideal alternative for
those seeking increased income. Yields are approximately 1.5%
above the 91-day T-Bill rate (near the three-year GIC rate, at
time of writing). The MBS represents an ownership interest in a
pool of National Housing Act insured, residential first
mortgages. The pool produces monthly cash flow which includes interest payments together with scheduled principal
payments. At the moment the MBS is available in a five-year
term only. These will suit the buyer of monthly-pay GICs or
those who are considering annuities. Others will be frustrated by
the payback of capital.

Preferred Shares

Before leaving a discussion of income-generating instruments, a word on preferred shares and tax reform. For
many years, taxable investors who were looking for increased
income with little more risk have turned to preferred shares. The
dividend tax credit has made this advisable. Two recent reductions to the dividend tax credit have left some advantage to dividend income over interest income on an after-tax basis.
However, the uncertainty caused by these reductions makes an
elimination of the tax credit for dividends seem likely. So the
risk of holding preferreds for income alone is probably too great
for the marginal advantage gained. Tax reform proposals which
are very new as this is being written would seem to inhibit the
issue of preferreds by non-taxable corporations. It is too early
to state emphatically that the retractable preferred share will
soon be a thing of the past. It is certain, however, that tax
reform will significantly influence our investment choices.
Those of you who have already taken the $100,000 lifetime
capital gains exemption should look carefully at the relative
after-tax returns of dividends, interest and capital gains. It

would appear at first glance that dividend income may be more advantageous than capital gains. For you the existing retractable and straight preferred shares may be worth the "government" risk.

The tax reform measures introduced in June, 1987 are more complex than they appear on the surface and they may well be changed before the proposals are implemented. As an astute investor interested in real return, you must be well informed on matters of taxation. After-tax yield should be a part of your thinking but please don't take unreasonable risks just to avoid taxation.

Convertible Preferreds and Convertible Debentures

Convertible preferreds and convertible debentures are thought by many to offer the best of both worlds — a good yield, reasonable safety from market volatility and capital gains potential. Others will be frustrated at their slow movement.

As the name suggests, a convertible carries the right of conversion into the common stock of the issuing corporation. The number of shares which may be obtained is set at issue.

In May of 1987 Alberta Energy Corporation issued $100,000,000 Convertible Debentures due June 30, 2002. These were issued carrying a 6.75% interest rate (91-day T-Bills were yielding 8.25% at the time). The debentures are convertible into the common shares of AEC at any time up to June 30, 1997 at a conversion premium of 16.1% over the price of the common stock at issue date. In other words, each $100.00 debenture could be converted into 42.78 shares of AEC common stock. At the end of June, 1987, the debenture was selling at $102.00, a premium of $2.00 per $100.00, reflecting a $1.00 rise in the common stock since the issue of the debenture. Alberta Energy common now pays a dividend of 30 cents per share, a yield after tax that is well below that of the debenture. The debenture therefore is protected on the downside by its yield while the common is not. The debenture will decline only to the point at which it could not be purchased for a yield comparable to to straight (non-convertible) bonds of equivalent quality. The other side of the coin is, however, that the stock has risen 5% and the debenture only 2% in the same length of time.

If AEC common continues to rise, the debenture will continue to rise, and the disparity in percentage increases will diminish until the debenture begins to act just like the stock. At this point you will probably sell the debenture unless you think that the stock has further room to grow and that conversion into the common would make sense.

Convertibles, of course, are not foolproof. A rapid rise in interest rates can leave the interest yield non-competitive and damage the ability of the issuing corporation to grow. However, those with the long view who choose quality issues will find them satisfying, but traders will be bored.

GROWTH OF CAPITAL

If income from your capital is not of prime concern to you, you have an ever-growing menu of capital gains vehicles available to you through the markets of the world. Let's start with mutual funds.

Mutual Funds

For many, mutual funds offer the hands-off capital gain potential they desire. A good equity fund (a stock fund as opposed to a bond or a balanced fund) will have first class management and will have returned approximately 20% on average over the last 10 years. This return will be a mixture of dividend and capital gain and will assume reinvested dividends. On average is stressed because you must understand that any fund can go down and negative returns are not unusual. Recent returns on internationally invested funds have been much better than those invested within Canada and this can be expected to continue.

Get a copy of the *Financial Times* survey of mutual funds. Your library will carry this financial weekly. An hour spent with the survey will reveal differences in composition and volatility. The *Financial Post* has an annual survey of year-to-year performance of funds registered for sale in Canada. Having read all this you will understand that past performance is no guarantee of future performance. However, past performance in relation to other funds will be one of the few guides you will have in making your decision.

As a new buyer you should be aware of the investment objective of the fund. This will be set out in the first few pages of the prospectus. Needless to say, the objective of the fund must match your objective. No sense in buying a fund whose objective is to take risks on emerging markets if you want to avoid risk.

The prospectus will also set out commission charges. There are many changes to mutual fund commissions going on now — no-load funds are adding commissions and funds are appearing with no buying fee but with a selling charge which reduces to zero if the fund is held 10 years. Whereas an 8.5% entry fee with no redemption fee was once standard, 5% now seems to be accepted.

There is an increasing number of sector funds available — Gas and Energy, High Tech, Europe, Japan, Health, etc. There are certainly times when investment in these funds makes sense, but that is the point. You will have to know when that time arrives (and departs). This requires a certain degree of market sophistication and attention. The average mutual fund buyer would do well to stick to funds that have a wider market objective.

And now to the really interesting stuff.

Building a Stock Portfolio

For many people the purchase of their first stock can be a world-opening experience. The health of your company can be affected by factors as diverse as the weather and the degree of political tension in the far East. Of course you are not required to become an expert on either the weather or the far East to purchase a stock — that's up to the management of your company. You have, however, bought a window on a wider world and you can look through it if and when you feel the urge. No amount of study alone will convince you about the wonders and the advantages of investing in the stock market — eventually you will have to take some of your very own money and buy a stock.

It will take you a year or two to get the feel for the rhythm of the market and to understand its strengths and weaknesses. I have not seen a book yet that will make you infallible in your choices of stocks. Everyone makes mistakes occasionally. As you embark on building a portfolio over the years ahead you can take comfort in the fact that over the last 116 years an investment in gold has doubled, money invested in short-term deposits has appreciated 8-fold, but capital invested in the stock market has grown more than 6000-fold. (Total returns deflated by the Consumer Price Index.)

You will see hills and valleys clearly. What is less apparent is the long-term market rise. All those glorious statistics that illustrate market gains assume reinvested dividends. In fact up to 80% of the increase can be attributed to dollar cost averaging by reinvested dividends over the long term. That is to say that if your dividends are used to buy more shares you will have the advantage of buying more when the price is low and more as the dividends increase.

When you buy a stock you will be asked to state your objective. How much risk are your prepared to take? Let's assume that you are prepared to accept different levels of risk in different proportions and that over the next five years you plan to build a portfolio of stocks. (Most portfolio building articles are concerned with the proportion of money divided among stocks, bonds and cash.)

You will begin by looking at the overall economic environment, which, by the way always look bleak to the novice. Many would-be investors have stayed out of the market because they felt it was too high, that economic conditions were terrible, and that the market was due for a correction. As I write this in early July, 1987, some have been waiting for two years. They have waited through some dramatic market increases. Yes, the market is higher than it was last year. Would you be thinking of buying stocks if they only went down? What will protect you in the long run will be quality, diversity and averaging. Timing will be important later in your investing career when you have absorbed the rhythm of the market.

For starters look to accumulating about four stocks as a portfolio core. Look for traditional blue chips. You are looking for solid, non-cyclical companies that have demonstrated the ability to grow with the economy, and in bad economic times to outperform the economy. Your accumulation of these stocks will not be all at one time so you can take advantage of market swings.

Of course, you will look for opportunities to reinvest your dividends. Most of the major companies offer this opportunity to buy full and/or partial shares at the market price when each dividend is declared. You will be surprised and pleased at how quickly you build up your holdings.

Sometimes you will pay more and sometimes less for your market favourites. When you have accumulated say 300-500 shares of your market favourites you are in a position to branch out. By this time you will be fearless — having survived inflation, tax reform, good times and bad. You've seen your favourites rise and fall, be loved and hated by the analysts, but convinced that good management was in place, you held on.

Obviously a portfolio has to be weeded at times. Companies change and fail and are taken over, but unless you want to become a trader, benign neglect has a lot to be said for it as a market strategy — if you have chosen your stocks well in the first place. Such a strategy is placing faith in the country and the economy and the ability of the management to grow.

As your level of sophistication rises, and as your friends tell you about all the money they have made in gold, oil, etc., you will become aware that stocks don't all rise and fall at the same time. Sectors advance and retreat as the short-term economic conditions change. You are now ready to add some cyclical stocks to your portfolio. You will also be taking more risk as your objective has become more short-term in this portion of your portfolio. You will take your profits (or losses) as the economic conditions conducive to the growth of this sector change. You can waste a lot of time at this stage looking for undervalued situations. Indeed there are often bargains for those who will spend the time in comparative analysis. I would advise you to simply buy the best oil, gold, forest product, etc. stock, although these will usually be the higher priced stocks, and let the trend carry you.

Now you have four core stocks and perhaps two cyclicals and maybe you're ready for more risk. And please note that this part comes later in your investing career, not early. Ten percent of your assets can be set aside for high risk if you are financially secure. If you just want to have fun, then seek out a broker who specializes in high-risk investments and bet your 10% on the penny stocks. This is a market fueled by rumour and expectation and is short on facts and seldom has earnings. There are straight exploration plans and idea/concept stocks. Many people throw money at this part of the market. Surely however, the guiding principle should be to take as little risk as possible even in the high-risk arena. Many, many new idea stocks, new product stocks and exploration plays are available to the Canadian investor. Among them there will be many short-term winners, and there will be some long-term winners as well. This is an area where you will not get much help from your broker. Brokerage houses cannot provide research opinions on all stocks and must, of necessity, limit themselves to the "big cap" stocks. So you're on your own here unless you can find a broker who specializes. You may find one or more of the many stock-picking newsletters helpful.

Many novice investors are drawn to the turn-around situation. These are companies that have experienced great difficulty and may be on the verge of bankruptcy or reorganization — Varity, Geac, Dome Petroleum, to name just three. I think that the attraction is that the prices are so low that they have to go up — well, don't they? Maybe. The risk here is very high and the only reasonable way to handle the risk is through diversification. If you are drawn to this type of stock as many of us are, please buy about 10 different ones so that the big winners can compensate for the ones that become wallpaper. The time it takes for a stock that has been close to death to recover is often years longer than the investor anticipates. Just ask all those who hold Varity (formerly Massey Ferguson).

New Issues

New issues may be initial public offerings in that the stock has never traded publicly before or additional treasury stock of a stock that already trades. Before you, as an investor, buy any new issue you must determine if the stock suits your investment objectives. When markets are good, companies are anxious to raise equity capital and the new issues will be so abundant that no one can be an authority.

All new issues will be priced in the context of the market — the price to the public will probably be somewhat below comparable stocks on a price/earnings multiple for initial public offerings and perhaps an eighth below the close of the stock already trading. Of course in both these cases the commission is born by the seller (the company), not you, the buyer.

Many initial public offerings are those of companies with long histories whose financial statements for a whole business cycle are available. These issues merit your consideration. Issues of lesser quality are best left on the shelf. Aside from market recognition, or lack of it, which may cause your new issue to remain in the dumps for a long, long time, the company's products may be untried or non-existent. Projected earnings are just that, projected, not actual. So, buyer beware.

Foreign Investing

The internationalization of the world's stock markets is here. Canadians have become familiar with off-shore new issues as they have taken part in the privitization going on in Britain. The elaborate and successful marketing efforts that accompanied the public offering of British Telecom set the stage for other companies to issue stock on the world stage.

While this is very exciting, the hazards of currency fluctuation give trading and investing internationally an added edge of uncertainty. However, Canadian markets have lagged the markets of the world and true diversity in investing would demand some international exposure. This is an area where the internationally invested mutual fund is a must.

As I write this you will find that the international funds have greatly increased their exposure to North America in recognition of the very high price/earnings multiples in the far East. For comparison, to June, 1987, the Canadian market had risen 20.6% over the last 52 weeks, the Australian market 51%, Japan 50.7%, Singapore 70%. Over the same period the markets of Holland, Sweden and Switzerland had underperformed the Canadian market. If you are holding Canadian mutual funds or Canadian stocks you may wish to find an international mutual fund that is not heavy in Canadian stocks.

Special Situations

The "special situation" deserves some explanation. As you will quickly become aware, the market is earnings driven — that is, a stock will generally go up if there is a perception that its earnings are going to increase in the year ahead. (As the market always anticipates, there are times when the short-term earnings are going to be exceptionally good, but longer-term they may be weak. In these cases you will be frustrated by your stock's refusal to go up.)

Analysts are constantly on the lookout for stocks whose earnings (or potential earnings) in some special circumstances are or could go up dramatically — out of proportion to others in the sector. The circumstances can be diverse — increased gold reserves, takeovers, asset sales, demographic shifts, cost control and fluctuations in commodity prices, etc. The experienced investor may want to commit an increasing amount of assets to these situations as the rewards can be great. Certainly you would not want to make a commitment to a stock whose earnings you thought would go down.

As a beginner, however, attention to the often mind boggling projections may divert you from your goal of building a long-term core portfolio.

YOU AND YOUR BROKER

Barriers between financial institutions are falling fast and soon brokerage houses will not be alone in offering full brokerage services. Banks with discount services are becoming more prominent. A broker in a full-service house is a source of information, research and advice. Discount brokerages do transactions alone. Feel free to use either service, but do not take the time of a full-service broker if you plan to do your transactions through a discount broker.

Every broker has a specialty. Although most will claim to be generalists, the world of stocks and bonds is too big to do everything well. Find a broker with whom you feel comfortable for you will be making decisions together. Making market decisions should not be a passing process, although the process will become much easier as you and your broker get to know each other well. Some brokers never make suggestions unless asked. One wonders how they ever make any money. Some get upset when you don't take their advice. My own attitude is that clients should be alerted to what is available. This means occasional calls regarding new products, new issues, market trends, portfolio changes, tax shelters and special situations.

As a novice you may be embarrassed by your lack of knowledge. As always, the failure to ask foolish questions will lead to foolish mistakes. If your broker cannot take enough time to answer questions, find another. It is a fact of life that at the beginning of your investing you will be a small client and as brokers live on commissions you can expect them to spend the bulk of their time on the clients who pay the rent. Most, however, will be willing to talk at greater length after market hours.

You will find that the best way to build your market knowledge is to read the business section of the newspaper on a regular basis. The best daily business section in Canada is that of the *Globe and Mail*. Each Monday they feature a recommendation on one Canadian and one U.S. stock. By reading analysis such as this you will soon become familiar with investment terms and standards. Good luck.

CHAPTER 8

LEGAL AIDS

By Karen Selick

INTRODUCTION

While the other chapters of this book have focussed primarily on how to make money, this chapter will deal with the legal aspects of making, keeping and finally disposing of your wealth.

What follows is a "grab-bag" of legal tips and caveats in various areas. These are things that I, as a lawyer, tell my clients on a daily basis. Some will help you avoid costly lawsuits. Some will help you save money on taxes. Some will help you avoid "false economy" — you'll learn when to spend a little bit of money in order to save a lot.

FAMILY LAW

At least one in three Canadian marriages ends in divorce. Not many people plan it that way, but it happens far too often to be ignored. A divorce can have disastrous financial consequences for several reasons:

- Your spouse may walk away with property which you always considered to be yours.
- It's a lot more expensive to maintain two separate households than it is to maintain two adults in the same household.
- If you spend too much time fighting to prevent losing property to your spouse, you'll lose it to your lawyer instead.

Marriage contracts used to be rare in Canada, except in the province of Quebec. Now, though, with the dramatic change that has taken place in the family law in most provinces over the past 15 years, more and more people are learning that a contract is the best way to protect themselves financially in the case of marriage breakdown.

In most provinces, a marriage contract can be used to avoid the application of the general provincial family law. For example, in Ontario, the law generally provides that upon marriage breakdown the poorer of the two spouses is entitled to a cash payment from the richer spouse in an amount which will equalize the increase in wealth of each spouse since the date of marriage. A well-drafted marriage contract can nullify this requirement entirely, and let each spouse keep his or her property entirely separate from the other's.

For those who were already married at the time such legislation was enacted, there is unfortunately not much possibility of relief, unless your spouse agrees to a marriage contract now. However, there is no reason to expect a spouse who will benefit from the new law to give up his or her newly acquired rights and enter into a contract merely because you ask. Obviously, the best time to arrange for a marriage contract is before you tie the knot.

Nevertheless, if you fear that your marriage may be headed for trouble, there are steps you can take now which will help you in the future. The family law of many provinces makes some allowance for property owned by each spouse at the date of marriage. The longer you are married, the more difficult it becomes to remember exactly what you owned at the date of marriage, and to establish a reasonable value for that property. To protect yourself, you can start right now to:

- compile a list of your pre-marriage property,
- document your list by preserving bank passbooks, bills of sale, etc.,
- obtain appraisals as of the date of marriage for those items whose value you cannot otherwise establish.

Another step you can take if you are already married is to spend half an hour or more consulting a good family law lawyer to learn exactly what the law is in your province and how it might affect you. The law is generally riddled with exceptions which can be used to your advantage — but only if you know about them in time. For example, in Ontario, property acquired during the marriage by gift or inheritance does not have to be split with your spouse, provided that it is still in its original form, or can be traced directly to a replacement asset, at the date of separation. Thus, if you inherit cash and keep it in a separate bank account or even a separate brokerage account, you won't have to divide it when you split up; but if you sink your inherited cash into a jointly owned house or joint account, you can expect to lose half of it.

There are usually provisions in the law granting special treatment for a matrimonial home. A knowledgeable lawyer can explain what these are in your province and suggest ways of legally avoiding or mitigating their effect.

If you do end up separated or divorced, it is wise to have a separation agreement prepared. There are often tax consequences attached to dividing up joint property or making support payments to an estranged spouse or child. For the purposes of the Income Tax Act, joint elections may have to be filed. All of these things, if inserted into a properly worded agreement or court order, can save you money.

REAL ESTATE

The purchase or sale of real estate is one area where seeing a lawyer at the right time can prevent a lot of problems and save you money. The time to see your lawyer is before you sign the offer, not after. Most lawyers base their fee for real estate deals on the value of the property, rather than on the time they spend, except in an unusually complicted cased requiring a great deal more time than normal. Therefore, it should not cost you any more to have your lawyer inspect your offer before you sign it. In fact, if he or she can correct a problem before the offer becomes a completed agreement of purchase and sale, this will prevent your deal from becoming the unusual, time-consuming one which warrants additional legal fees.

If you live in a major city, it may help to deal with a lawyer who is especially familiar with the part of town where your real estate is located. There are parts of Toronto which have termite problems, for example. A lawyer who deals regularly with property in those neighbourhoods will probably suggest a termite inspection clause in your offer to purchase, whereas a lawyer in a different part of the city may not be aware of the need for such a clause.

Whether you're buying residential real estate or commercial, it's always a good idea to pay for a structural inspection by a reputable firm, unless you yourself have considerable expertise in the field of construction. Your lawyer can insert a clause in your offer making it conditional upon a satisfactory inspection report. For a fee of a few hundred dollars the inspectors can tell you about major and minor defects in the building. If the problems are significant, you may decide to back out of the deal entirely. If there are a number of minor problems which can be repaired to your satisfaction, you may wish to negotiate for a reduction in the price. Either way, the inspection can easily pay for itself.

If you're selling, it is often wise to consult your lawyer even before you sign a real estate agent's listing agreement. Many standard form agreements contain a clause which makes you liable for the agent's commission whether or not you actually complete the sale of your house. There are all sorts of reasons why a deal may fall through, and not all of them involve any fault on your part. Make sure you do not get caught having to pay an agent if your transaction can't be completed for one reason or another.

STARTING UP A SMALL BUSINESS

When you are planning to start a small business, one of the first choices you will want to consider is the organizational structure. If you will be the only person involved in the business, it can remain a sole proprietorship. If there will be others involved, you can set up as a partnership. On the other hand, you may wish to incorporate; this can be done regardless of the number of people involved.

There are both tax and non-tax factors to consider. Among the tax factors are the following:

- From time to time, various levels of government may offer incentives to new corporations. At the time of writing, the Ontario government is giving a three-year tax holiday to newly incorporated companies, provided certain conditions are met. In most cases, this will make it more profitable to operate as a corporation than otherwise. Numerical comparisons can be done for other provinces if their tax rates are known.
- If your new business might suffer losses over the first few years, you should be careful to incorporate at the right time, or the ability to carry those losses over against profitable years may be lost. If you have other income as an individual against which the business losses can be offset, you may not wish to incorporate. But if the business losses can only be off-

set by future business income, do not make the mistake of waiting until the business is profitable before incorporating — the pre-incorporation losses will go unused forever.
- If family members will be assisting you in the business, it may be wise to incorporate. Just as your tax bill can be lowered through the use of the dividend gross-up and tax credit rather than direct business income, the same advantage is available to a spouse or child who receives dividends rather than salary.

There are other reasons besides tax, however, why you may wish to incorporate:

- Incorporation means that you, as a shareholder, will have limited liability for the obligations and actions of the corporation. If you have other assets which are not going to be involved in the business and which you wish to protect, incorporation may be the answer. It is not a universal solution, however. Financial institutions advancing money to your company will probably insist on a personal guarantee from you.
- Many people feel that there is some prestige associated with a corporation.
- Incorporation imparts a sense of grandeur and continuity to those dealing with the business. Realistic or not, many people are more satisfied to deal with a corporation than with an individual.

If you choose to operate in partnership with other individuals, it is highly recommended that you consult a lawyer and have a partnership agreement prepared. If you incorporate with other shareholders, a shareholders' agreement can provide for many of the same things that a partnership agreement would deal with. The preparation of such an agreement can save a lot of grief and a lot of money when crucial events occur which you didn't think about in the excitement of setting up the new business.

One of the most important things to consider is what would happen in the event of your death or the death of one of your partners or other shareholders. You may wish to bind yourselves to an agreement which will provide for an option to the surviving shareholder to buy the interest in the business from the estate of the deceased person at a price fixed by formula. In that case, you should also consider buying life insurance on each other so that the survivors will be able to meet their obligations to purchase. Opinions vary as to whether it is better for the insurance policies to be owned by the business or by the shareholders or partners individually. The decision will be affected by both tax considerations and family law considerations. Your decision should be made only after consulting an insurance professional and a lawyer.

Another important event which your agreement should provide for is the possibility of a partner or shareholder wanting to depart from the business in a manner other than by death. There are many ways of handling this, ranging from the shotgun buy-sell agreement, to the formula pricing method, to having an annual valuation done.

With the current state of family law, you should be concerned about the marital status of anyone with whom you intend to be engaged in business. If your partner's marriage breaks up, you could suddenly find yourself in business with both your partner and his spouse. It may be necessary for everyone involved to have a marriage contract prepared before any risks are taken.

Employees are another source of potential problems. Sometimes they leave, setting up their own businesses in competition with yours, or taking valuable knowledge to a new job with one of your competitors. Have your employment contracts drafted by a lawyer familiar with the current developments in employment law. It is not wise to draft them yourself. You may think you have an iron-clad contract which will prevent your employees from competing with you or harming your business in any way, but you'll be extremely surprised and sorry to discover that this is precisely the wrong way to approach the problem. If your agreement effectively prevents a former employee from earning a livelihood, you may find that the restrictions will be deemed too broad by a court and will be thrown out entirely.

ESTATE AND WILL PLANNING

If you've gone to a lot of trouble to build your capital and save taxes during your lifetime, you will hate to see all that effort go down the drain when you die. Proper estate and will planning can help ensure that your spouse and children keep the benefits you've earned.

It is important to have a will prepared and periodically updated. You may believe you don't need a will because the law of intestacy will divide your property in much the same way as you would want it divided anyway. But a will does more than merely state how your property is to be divided. It also allows you to appoint an executor who will be responsible for settling your affairs. If an estate has no executor, the courts can appoint an administrator, but this is usually a more time-consuming and expensive process, and it may result in the appointment of someone other than the person you would have preferred.

An intestacy should especially be avoided if your children are still under the age of majority. Property left to a minor must be administered by the courts unless you have appointed someone as trustee under your will. Getting the money out of court, to use for orthodontal fees or other unexpected needs, will be more difficult and expensive than merely asking a sympathetic trustee.

It is generally best to have your will prepared by a lawyer. Some provinces now permit holograph wills (written entirely in the testator's handwriting), and it is of course always possible to buy a blank will form at a stationery store, write your own will and have it witnessed. The problem with these home-made wills is that they sometimes backfire. If your language is ambiguous, or if you forget an important clause, your estate could wind up as the subject of some lengthy and costly court proceedings. Most lawyers charge an extremely reasonable fee for preparing a will, and the expense is well justified by the peace of mind it will bring.

You should also have your will updated periodically, perhaps every five years or so. During that time there may be additions to or deaths in your family, a change in the assets you will have to dispose of, or changes in the law.

Probate fees can often be avoided by arranging for property to pass outside of your will. This can be done, for example, by owning real estate or bank accounts as joint tenants with a right of survivorship. Upon your death, the property automatically passes to the joint owner, regardless of the provisions of your will. (In some provinces, particularly Ontario, the rules of joint tenancy of real estate have been modified where the joint tenants are not spouses; check with your lawyer.)

Life insurance policies and RRSPs can in most provinces be passed outside your will by designating a beneficiary in writing with the insurance company or trustee of the plan, again saving probate fees.

There are also steps which can be taken to save income tax, particularly capital gains tax, on death. Property with an accrued gain at the time of your death can be left to a spouse on a "roll-over" basis: your spouse is deemed to have acquired the property at the amount it cost you, so that the capital gain is deferred until the surviving spouse either dies or disposes of the property. At the time of writing, there is an exemption from capital gains tax of $100,000 worth of gains. If this exemption continues in effect, it may be more beneficial for your executor to elect not to have the rollover apply.

An RRSP which is left to a spouse, either by designating your spouse as a beneficiary with the trustee or by leaving it to him or her in your will, is not subject to income tax on your death, as long as your spouse contributes to an RRSP in his or her own name. From that point on, it will be subject to the same tax treatment as any other RRSP funds.

If you will be leaving property in your will to married children, you may wish to get advice concerning the current state of family law in the province where your children reside. Ontario has recently enacted laws which can help to keep your bequests out of the hands of a son- or daughter-in-law, provided your will is worded appropriately.

Once your will is prepared, make sure your executor knows where it is being kept. To avoid any possible confusion, destroy all previous wills.

A COLLECTION OF TAX TIPS

Evasion or Avoidance: Get an Advance Ruling

There is an important difference between tax evasion and tax avoidance. Evasion is illegal. Evasion means doing things like not reporting all of your income, exaggerating your expenses, or claiming non-existent dependents. Tax evasion is dangerous. If you are caught, it can cost you two times the amount of tax "saved", plus interest and penalties. If it's serious enough, you can go to jail. It is definitely not recommended.

Tax avoidance, on the other hand, merely means arranging your affairs in such a way as to pay the minimum amount of tax legally required. Tax avoidance includes such commonplace acts as contributing to an RRSP or buying a tax shelter recommended by your stockbroker, but it can also include much more complex transactions. Not all tax avoidance plans are reliable in avoiding tax. What may seem workable to your tax advisor can be challenged by Revenue Canada. But if there is an honest dispute over the state of the law, the worst that can happen is that you will have to pay the back taxes and interest.

If you are proposing a complicated transaction, you can apply through a tax lawyer or accountant to have Revenue Canada give you an advance ruling. Your identity will not be revealed, but the details of the proposed transaction will be set out, together with your interpretation of the tax consequences. Revenue Canada will then tell you whether they agree or disagree with your interpretation. If their ruling is favourable, it is binding on them for that one transaction (although not necessarily for subsequent transactions, even if they are identical). You have to pay for Revenue Canada's time in preparing an advance ruling, so the procedure is usually used only for major transactions.

The provisions announced on June 18, 1987 by Finance Minister Michael Wilson included extensive measures to combat tax avoidance. Many tax specialists have expressed outrage at what they consider to be vague and arbitrary proposals. At this stage, it is impossible to know how the law will look when finally enacted.

Pay Tax On Time

Make every effort to file your tax return and to pay tax installments on time. Interest is charged on overdue payments. While the rate may be lower than you'd pay if you had to borrow the money at the bank, it is also non-deductible.

What To Do If You Are Reassessed

If Revenue Canada disagrees with something on your tax return and feels that you should be paying more tax, they will issue a form called a Notice of Reassessment. If you want to challenge their position, you must file a Notice of Objection. This must be done within 90 days of the date on the Notice of Reassessment. It is important not to miss this deadline, and it is astonishing how many people do. You may try negotiating with the District Taxation Office first, but do not be lulled into a false sense of security by ongoing negotiations. File the Notice of Objection within the time limit, then continue your talks. If no progress is made, get advice from a tax lawyer or accountant. The next step in your case is to have the matter heard by the Tax

Review Board, where you can represent yourself if you wish. However, unless you want to make a detailed study of the law, it may be wiser to have representation by someone familiar with the Income Tax Act and general tax jargon.

Partners and Proprietors: Choose Your Year-End Wisely

If you carry on business as a sole proprietor or a partnership, you can defer the payment of income tax by a perfectly legitimate method. The owner of a business is taxed on the business income in the calendar year in which the fiscal year of the business ends. Similarly, partners are taxed on their income from the partnership in the calendar year in which the fiscal year of the partnership ends.

By choosing a fiscal period which ends, for example, on January 31, 1988, you would include in your 1988 tax return the income for the period February 1, 1987 to January 31, 1988. You would not be liable for the final installment of tax on that income until April, 1989. On the other hand, if your fiscal year had ended one month earlier (that is, on December 31, 1987) you would include the income from January 1, 1987 to December 31, 1987 in your 1987 tax return, and pay your last installment of tax in April, 1988.

It is important to get this 11-month deferral in place immediately upon starting up your business. The deferral will continue each year that you are in business. If you are already operating with a less advantageous fiscal year end, you might try changing it if there are other reasons for doing so. Revenue Canada will not allow a change of year-end merely for the purpose of getting this deferral.

Reduce Tax Withheld At Source

If you work as an employee for someone else, you may think that your tax planning can only be done at the end of the year because your income tax is deducted from your salary each time you are paid. However, there are provisions in the Income Tax Act which allow your employer to reduce your deductions if you can satisfy Revenue Canada that you would otherwise suffer undue hardship.

Your withholding tax can be reduced if you are entitled to claim a deduction on your tax return for such things as support payments to an estranged spouse, medical expenses in excess of 3% of your net income, moving expenses, child care expenses, business losses or contributions to a group RRSP.

You apply by writing to the Source Deductions Department of your District Taxation Office. Explain why you will be entitled to the deduction and provide some evidence (such as a court order for support payments, or receipts for moving expenses).

The decision to reduce your withholding tax is entirely at the discretion of the District Taxation Office, but they have not in the past set a very high standard for undue hardship. If they find in your favour, they will write directly to your employer authorizing a reduction in your taxes.

Every Parent Can Income Split

One of the most widely used techniques for reducing taxes has been to split income among family members, who can then pay tax at a lower marginal rate. Over the past few years, the rules have become more and more strict about how income can and cannot be split, and it is now impossible to use many of the techniques which were formerly considered acceptable.

One method which has escaped the ever-tightening net is a simple technique which can be used by every parent whose children are under the age of 18. Simply deposit your child's family allowance (baby bonus) cheque in an account in the name of your child, and the interest earned on it will be taxed in your child's hands. This is an exception to the normal rules which attribute income from a gift to a child back to the parent, who must pay the tax on it. Note, though, that this is an administrative concession by Revenue Canada, and can be changed by them at any time.

Planning For Tax Reform

With the introduction of tax reform proposals on June 18, 1987, the Minister of Finance closed some existing tax benefits, but at the same time opened up new opportunities for tax saving. Because of the difference in timing between the introduction of reduced income tax rates and the new national sales tax, 1987 and 1988 may be banner years for saving tax.

The marginal tax rate for most people will fall from 1987 to 1988. This means that if you can find a way of deferring income until the later year, you will save money. This will be an especially important consideration for those choosing a year-end for a new business. You may be able to arrange a deferral of investment income by taking out compound interest instruments instead of something that pays annually. But be careful; this is a double-edged sword. In 1988, the $1,000 exemption for investment income will disappear. For some people, it will be more advantageous to accelerate investment income than to defer it.

If you are planning to purchase any major consumption items in the next few years (such as a car or large appliances), consider advancing your purchase before the new sales tax is implemented. Similarly, since the new tax is expected to be imposed on the sale of services (which are not currently taxed), now may be the time to get your teeth capped, your house landscaped, your will prepared, and so on.

CHAPTER 9

CONSUMER LAW

By Terry Wagar

INTRODUCTION

Sound investment strategies make money — knowing and exercising your legal rights may very well save you money. In this chapter, I am going to look at the broad area of contracts. This discussion will be followed by an analysis of the law relating to buying goods and services. Finally, I will outline what laws exist to protect the consumer and how to make a complaint if you choose to do so.

CONTRACT LAW

Most, if not all, of us have fallen into the trap of signing a contract without fully considering or understanding what our legal rights and responsibilities really are. Contrary to our better judgment, we tend to follow the instructions of the other party when told to "just sign here on the dotted line". How often have you actually taken the time to read the conditions which you are agreeing to?

We are continually making contracts, ranging from complex legal documents formally signed by the contracting parties to informal, unwritten arrangements between friends. A contract, which may be defined basically as "an agreement enforceable at law", must contain five essential elements.

Mutual Agreement (Offer and Acceptance)

As a starting point, a legally binding agreement requires the making of an offer (i.e., Mr. Jones offers to sell this car for $2,000) and acceptance of that offer (Mrs. Brown agrees to buy the car at that price). A valid offer must contain all of the necessary terms so as to enable the other party to determine precisely what is being offered and under what conditions.

Assuming an offer has been made, a contract comes into existence at the moment of acceptance. Unless specified otherwise, communication of acceptance is necessary and may be done by words or conduct.

As a general rule, a contract does not exist until the person making the offer knows that the other party has accepted his or her offer. However, there is one exception — when acceptance is made by mail, the "post box rule" states that acceptance occurs when the letter is put in the mail box.

Consideration or a Seal

A binding contract must either be for valuable consideration or under seal. In most situations, consideration ("the price for which the act or promise of the other part is bought") is present. However, it should be noted that the courts generally are not concerned with the adequacy or amount of the consideration but only whether valid consideration exists. For example, a contract to buy land for $1 is binding although the consideration is clearly inadequate.

Contracts under seal are less common and are used if required by law, for contracts where no consideration is desired, or when corporations formally sign their names.

Capacity to Contract

What happens if a person enters into a contract with a minor, a lunatic, or a drunkard? In the case of a contract with a minor (a person who has not yet attained the age of majority), the agreement is not enforceable against the minor but is enforceable by the minor against the adult. However, a minor is liable to pay a reasonable price for goods considered "necessaries" in relation to his station in life (i.e., food, clothing, shelter) and is bound to the terms of an employment contract deemed to be for his or her benefit.

Where a contract is made with a lunatic or a drunkard, the agreement is valid and binding unless it can be demonstrated that the individual was mentally incompetent or drunk (incapable of making a rational decision) and that the other party was aware of the condition.

Lawful Subject Matter

As a general principle, contracts for an illegal purpose are void — there is no binding agreement. Examples of illegal contracts include: an agreement to commit a crime or engage in an immoral performance, a contract which contravenes the sanctity of marriage, a wager, or a contract which may prejudice public safety or be in restraint of trade.

Intention to Create Binding Legal Relations

The parties must intend to be bound by the contract and the resulting legal consequences. In family arrangements where the parties are on friendly terms, the courts presume that there is no intention to create binding legal relations. However, the opposite presumption is true in commercial arrangements or in situations where the marriage has broken down and bargaining is keen.

SOME SPECIAL TYPES OF CONTRACTS

Personal Guarantees

Frequently, people agree to co-sign loans (that is, give personal guarantees) for their friends, relatives or business colleagues without understanding their rights and obligations. More than one friendship has been destroyed when a "can't lose" business proposition has failed and the lender has demanded payment from the person who co-signed the loan agreement.

What is a Personal Guarantee?

A party in the business of loaning money often is unwilling to do so if the only security is the borrower's promise to repay the money. Consequently, an individual may only be able to get financing if a third party (the "guarantor" or "co-signer") co-signs the loan on the borrower's behalf.

A third party who agrees to co-sign a loan promises to make the payments on the borrower's loan in the event that the borrower fails to do so and defaults on the loan. This promise is called a "personal guarantee".

For example, if one of your children persuades you to co-sign a bank loan, you are giving the bank a personal guarantee that you will make the scheduled payments in the event that your child fails to do so.

The Guarantor's Rights and Obligations

It should be noted that the co-signer's personal guarantee is made to the lender (i.e., a bank) who has no rights against him or her until the borrower defaults on the loan.

However, upon default by the borrower, the co-signer's obligation to make payments on the loan begins immediately — the lender does not have to sue the borrower first before recovering from the guarantor unless this is specifically provided for in the loan agreement. In other words, the bank may take action against you immediately if your child defaults on the loan.

It may be somewhat comforting to know that if the guarantor is required to pay off the loan, he may sue the borrower for the amount paid to the lender and for expenses arising from the default. However, in many cases the borrower may not have sufficient assets to justify legal action. In other words, the guarantor may have a legal right but no remedy.

Practical Considerations

Before signing a personal guarantee, be sure to evaluate the borrower's ability to make the loan payments. Is the proposed business or investment a sound proposition? How much faith do you have in the borrower? In the event that you have to pay off the loan, does the borrower have sufficient assets should you choose to sue? Are you ready, willing and able to meet the loan payments should the borrower default?

You should be aware that some loan agreements contain what is known as an "acceleration clause". If such a clause exists, the lender may demand immediate payment of the entire balance due.

Insurance Contracts

A discussion of the law of insurance is well beyond the scope of this chapter. As a result, I am not going to outline the law in any great detail but rather just mention some things to look for when purchasing insurance.

- Be sure to have your complete insurance needs carefully evaluated. A number of people have life, home and automobile insurance, but you may need other insurance protection (i.e., disability, mortgage, or liability insurance, etc.). It is critical that you fully understand what the insurance you are now carrying actually covers. I have seen situations where individuals forgot to insure their apartment (if they are renting) or their business.
- Take your time when looking over an insurance contract before signing your name. Make sure that you understand exactly what is and what is not covered. Insurance contracts frequently contain "exclusions" — your insurance company will not protect you against losses which are caused by events excluded under the contract. Be aware of these exclusions and, depending on your situation, consider more complete protection.
- Insurance contracts often limit the extent of the insurer's liability. Have your assets appraised on a regular basis and make sure that your possessions are adequately insured under the contract. For example, policies may limit the amount recoverable for cash or jewelery stolen from the home.
- Keep your insurance policies in a safe place (such as a safety deposit box).

SOME SUGGESTIONS BEFORE YOU SIGN ANY CONTRACT

From a practical perspective, the following guidelines may provide some assistance in dealing with contracts:

- Before signing any contract, be sure to read the entire contract and understand what you are agreeing to. Although this suggestion is just good common sense, I cannot emphasize too strongly that you follow it.
- Do not sign a contract without considering your rights and obligations. Many contracts are very complex and confusing documents. Whether you are purchasing a home, buying a car, obtaining insurance or making any other type of agree-

ment, feel free to take your time in examining the contract. There is no law requiring you to sign on the dotted line merely because some agent or salesperson tells you to do so.

- If you need more time to look over the contract, feel free to take it home with you. For contracts you do not understand, consider obtaining independent legal advice. You are not required to sign a contract merely because someone asks you to do so — you are the one who has to live with the agreement.
- If you sign a contract, don't forget to get a copy of the agreement. In the event that future problems may arise, you will have your own copy of the contract — without it, your legal position may be weakened (the other side may also have lost the agreement or altered its provisions).

To sum up, the time to determine your rights and responsiblities under a contract and assess the risks involved is before you sign the agreement.

PURCHASING GOODS AND SERVICES

Before you decide to purchase a good or service, the seller may make a number of statements or promises about the product. These representations are called "express terms" and they may be made orally, in a written contract, or in an advertisement. Such promises are binding on the seller; obviously, for your own protection it is very important to have such representations in writing.

If the seller does not keep his or her part of the deal, you will be able to claim damages. If the seller breaches a very important term of the contract (called a "condition"), you may be able to have the contract cancelled and also recover any damages you have suffered. However, if the seller basically lives up to the agreement but breaks a promise of minor importance (called a "warranty"), you cannot have the contract cancelled but may sue for damages.

By way of example, if you buy a printer which the dealer assures you is compatible with your computer and you find out that the printer will not work with your system, then you may return the printer, get your money refunded, and sue for any damages you incurred based on the dealer's promise. On the other hand, if you discover that the printer will work just fine with your system but needs a $5 cable, then you will not be able to cancel the contract but would be able to recover damages for any loss that you suffered.

Implied Terms in a Contract of Sale

In addition to the express terms which a seller may agree to, there are a number of "implied terms" in consumer sales. The laws in each province are different and thus it is necessary to refer to the appropriate legislation (Sale of Goods Act, Consumer Protection Act or Consumer Product Warranty Act) in your province of residence. Nevertheless, the following provisions are customarily found across Canada:

- The seller must have clear title to the goods. If you buy stolen goods, the original owner is entitled to reclaim the goods. If the seller does not own the goods, you can cancel the contract and recover any damages; unfortunately, individuals who deal in stolen merchandise are frequently not around when you discover what has happened and want to sue them.
- The goods must be free of any financial claims (such as a mortgage) and no other person should be entitled to use the goods without your consent.
- If you buy goods by description, then the goods must correspond with the description. For example, if you buy something from a catalogue, there is an implied condition that the product conforms to the description.
- If the seller is told why you are buying the goods and you rely on his or her expertise, there is an implied condition that the goods are "reasonably fit for the purpose". There are two exceptions to this rule. Firstly, if you request a product by its brand name, then the rule does not apply. Secondly, the rule does not hold if the seller is not in the business of selling such goods (i.e., you buy a product from an individual after seeing an advertisement in the classified ads).
- The goods must be of "merchantable quality" if purchased from a dealer. It should be emphasized that if you buy a product from a store, there is no obligation required of the store to take the product back unless it is defective. In order to maintain good customer relations, most stores will allow refunds or exchanges; however, they are not bound by law to do so.
- If the sale of goods was by sample, then the rest of the goods must correspond with the sample you looked at.

- If you purchase a service, it must be performed in a skillful manner, and the person providing the service must exercise "reasonable care".

It should be noted that the above protections apply to the retail sale of new goods and the seller cannot contract out of these obligations. However, if used goods are being sold, the seller may (and frequently does) add a clause to the contract which removes some or all of the implied terms. Although there are some exceptions (for example, Saskatchewan's Consumer Product Warranty Act), the rules generally do not extend to manufacturers.

Buying a Car and Getting it Repaired

Thinking of buying a car? Planning to take your car in for repairs? If you are like most people, buying a car or taking your car in for repairs still makes you a little uneasy.

Buying a Car

Assuming that you have made the decision to buy a car, you must consider whether you want to make the purchase from a car dealer or from a private individual. It must be emphasized that the contract you agree to is only as good as the party you are dealing with.

Before you even consider signing an agreement, take the car for a test drive. If you are buying a used car, think about having your mechanic examine the vehicle.

If you decide that you want the car, it is critical that you determine who actually owns the car and whether there are any outstanding claims (such as mechanics' liens, conditional sales contracts and chattel mortgages).

If you buy a car from someone who is not the rightful owner, the car goes back to the person who actually owns the car — only the true owner can transfer good title.

I cannot emphasize too much the importance of carefully reading the contract of sale before signing. Make sure that you fully understand what you are agreeing to and do not be pressured into signing a document — you are the one that has to live with it. If necessary, insist on taking the agreement home or have your lawyer look it over.

If you are trading in an old car, be sure to clarify when the title to the car will pass from you to the dealer. The party holding the title is responsible for insurance coverage.

Be sure to obtain a written copy of the agreement (bill of sale) for your records. Do not leave without it.

Manufacturers' Warranties

Car manufacturers offer varying amounts of protection in their warranty agreements. Typically, manufacturers' warranties cover replacement parts and labor costs on the various items covered under the agreement. Historically, the protection was for one year or 20,000 kilometres (whichever came first), but extended warranty programs which are now available from several car manufacturers provide protection for considerably longer periods of time.

Be sure to examine exactly what is covered under the warranty protection plan. If you are interested in extended protection, inquire about the cost.

Each province has legislation such as the Sale of Goods Act or Consumer Protection Act which provides some protection to people purchasing cars. Such laws require that the goods are "reasonably fit" for their intended purpose. As well, if the person selling the goods is in the business of doing so, there is an implied condition that the goods are of "merchantable quality". However, be aware that the sellers of used cars frequently have a clause in the bill of sale which waives these protections.

Repairing Your Car

Unfortunately, cars have a habit of breaking down at times. If you are like most people, you don't enjoy taking your car in for repairs.

It is best to ask for an estimate before authorizing any repairs. You might also want to make clear to the garage to notify you before repairing your car if the bill is going to exceed the estimate. As a general rule, an "estimate" is not legally binding on the parties but it does give you some protection.

It should be noted that if you refuse to pay your repair bill, the garage may keep possession of your car under a mechanic's or repairer's lien.

If you do run into problems, you may want to contact a consumer protection agency (such as the Better Business Bureau) or consider an action in Small Claims Court.

As an aside, the Canadian Automobile Association provides members with a listing of garages who are willing to give estimates and will also help in resolving disputes between members and garages approved by the Association.

Buying on Credit

Before deciding to buy anything on credit, it goes without saying that you should carefully look at your particular financial situation and determine if you can afford the purchase.

If you want to obtain credit cards or borrow money, it is essential that you establish a good credit rating. Your credit rating, which is kept on file at a local credit bureau, basically shows the debts you have and whether you have paid your bills on a regular basis.

Over the past 20 years, every province has introduced laws protecting consumers who choose to buy on credit. For example, you are entitled to see your credit rating file. If your file contains information which you feel is misleading or incorrect, the credit bureau is required to remove that information unless it can show that the information is true.

Provincial laws also require that a person borrowing money must be given a written statement outlining the total amount of money received on credit, the rate of interest, and how additional charges will be calculated.

What If You Can't Pay?

If you fail to pay a bill on time, the party which has given you the credit generally sends you a reminder asking you to pay the money immediately. Late payment frequently requires an additional charge and thus it is advisable to pay your bills by the due date.

If you do not respond to the reminder letter, the borrower tends to get a bit more upset and sends out a less friendly letter emphasizing not only the amount of the late-payment charge but also the fact that failure to pay may seriously damage your credit rating.

It should be noted that you may be taken to court for failing to pay your bills. However, in most cases your account is turned over to a collection agency first. Collection agencies must be licenced or registered, and provincial laws restrict the methods they may use in collecting debts. For example, they are not permitted to threaten or harass the borrower, and they may not attempt to collect the debt from the debtor's family.

In addition, they are not entitled to discuss the matter with the borrower's employer (unless consent is given) other than to verify employment. As well, there are restrictions on when agencies may attempt to contact debtors. For example, calls between 9 p.m. and 8 a.m. or calls on Sunday are not allowed in Nova Scotia. Restrictions vary depending on the province of residence.

It must be emphasized that help is readily available for people falling into debt. In addition to counselling from people such as a banker, accountant or financial adviser, help is available from the Department of Consumer Affairs in your province. As a last resort, a debtor may declare personal bankruptcy.

PROTECTION FOR THE CONSUMER

Door-to-Door Sales

Although the law typically does not allow an individual to change his or her mind and cancel an agreement without being liable for breach of contract, consumers purchasing products or services from door-to-door salesmen receive special protection. It is believed that consumers are often exploited by door-to-door sellers and therfore, each province has enacted legislation permitting individuals to cancel contracts signed at home (within certain time limitations).

Depending upon the province in which the buyer resides, he or she is entitled to a "cooling off" period ranging from two to 10 days. During this period, a consumer may cancel the contract by notifying the seller (registered mail is advised) of his or her intention to do so. Upon cancellation of the agreement, the consumer is required to return any goods received and is entitled to recover any money (a deposit or down payment) previously paid to the seller.

It should be noted that the length of the "cooling-off" period, the notification of cancellation requirements, and the protections available vary noticeably among the provinces. One is advised to examine the relevant consumer protection or direct sales legislation in his or her province of residence.

Unsolicited Goods and Credit Cards

It has become a common practice of a number of companies to send unsolicited goods or credit cards through the mail. Once again, your liability and responsibility depends on the specific laws of your province.

With reference to unsolicited goods, the law in most provinces allows an individual receiving unsolicited goods to keep and use the goods without having to pay for them. As well, there is no obligation to return the goods to the sender or take special care of them.

With regard to unsolicited credit cards, the rules vary considerably among the provinces. Some jurisdictions make it unlawful to issue unsolicited credit cards (i.e., Alberta, Manitoba, New Brunswick, P.E.I. and Quebec). Other provinces provide that the recipient (or intended recipient) is not liable for transactions made unless he or she writes the card issuer accepting responsibility for the card or uses it to make purchases. My advice is to immediately cut up any unsolicited credit cards unless you want to use them.

Misleading Advertising

Sellers are constantly using a variety of advertising techniques in an attempt to convince us to purchase their particular product or service. While most advertisements are perfectly legal, methods of promotion designed to mislead the public are prohibited by law.

What Types of Advertising are Misleading?

Misleading or false advertising is specifically dealt with under the federal Combines Investigation Act. Under this legislation, the following types of advertising are prohibited by law:

Misleading Advertising With Respect to Price. It is an offence to advertise a product or service at a price below that which is actually charged the customer. However, the Act recognizes that mistakes in advertising are sometimes innocent; in such cases, the seller is permitted to correct the mistake by promptly placing another advertisement correcting the price in the original advertisement.

The practice of placing two prices on a product ("double ticketing") is not prohibited, but the seller is obligated to sell the item at the lower price. As well, it is unlawful to offer a free item with the purchase of a particular product (i.e., "buy one, get one free") and raise the price of the regular item to cover the additional cost.

Misleading Advertising With Respect to Statement of Fact. Advertisements used to promote a good or service must not contain misleading statements of fact designed to deceive the purchaser. For example, a cereal box contains the following words: "Free Gift Inside". Upon opening the package, you discover that you must send three box tops to receive the free gift. Such a promotion technique is prohibited.

Bait and Switch Selling. In an attempt to lure customers to the store, some sellers advertise items at bargain prices. Consumers may arrive at the store to find the lower-priced item has been replaced or switched with a higher-priced item. This practice is illegal unless the seller can prove that he had a reasonable quantity of the bargain-priced products on hand or that the inadequate supply was due to factors beyond his control. Some stores have a rain-check policy or offer to sell a product of equal or higher value at the bargain price — if the bargain-priced item is out of stock, feel free to ask about the store's particular policy.

Untested Warranties or Guarantees About the Product. An advertiser who makes any claim or promise about the performance or usable life of a product must bear the onus of establishing that the claim or promise was based on adequate and proper tests. When testing a particular product, it is not necessary that every item tested meet the claim. However, it has been suggested that not less than 95% of the items should meet the standard.

What Remedies Are Available?

If you feel that an advertisement is misleading, contact the federal Department of Consumer and Corporate Affairs. The Department will investigate your complaint and decide whether to charge the advertiser with violating the Combines Investigation Act. However, the process is not designed to compensate you but rather to protect the public at large from misleading advertising. You might also consider complaining to the Advertising Standards Council in your particular region.

It is also possible to sue the advertiser for damages suffered as a result of the misleading advertising. A civil action resulting from an alledged breach of the Act is possible, but because the law is somewhat complex and uncertain, it is advisable to seek legal counsel before pursuing this remedy.

In addition, sellers typically want to avoid bad publicity, and you may be able to negotiate an acceptable solution to the problem.

HOW TO MAKE YOUR COMPLAINT

All of us run into situations where we simply are not pleased with the product or service we purchased. The question is: What can be done about it?

The Phone Call or Personal Visit

In most situations, the best way to start griping is by means of a telephone call or personal visit. Although I prefer the personal visit, there may be times when it is not practical or appropriate.

If the company has a complaints department, ask for it. Otherwise, try to speak with someone of higher authority — do not be easily deterred when told by a salesclerk that "nothing can be done and the manager is not available".

Prior to making your call or visit, it is important to think about your plan of action. You should consider the following points:

* Whom do you want to speak with? Make sure that the person you are talking to has the authority to help you.
* Prepare in advance what you want. The time to think about what you hope to obtain is before you make your call or visit.
* Try and get a straightforward and specific reply. You should have already thought about your next move if given the runaround.
* Be sure to get the name of the person who spoke with you. This is important if you are not satisfied with the result.

Sending a Letter

If the phone call or personal visit is unsuccessful, you might consider sending a consumer letter. A good letter should not be too long (in most situations, one page is enough). The letter should get to the point, explain the problem, and outline what you want in compensation.

Although there is often a strong temptation to write a mean and nasty letter, such an approach may only complicate the problem. As well, it may be embarrassing to have the letter introduced as evidence if the matter goes to court.

In many situations, it is necessary to support your letter with such material as your sales receipt or a copy of the warranty or contract. Do not send the original copies with the letter; enclose photocopies if such material is necessary.

Third Party Assistance

In addition to taking action by yourself, you should consider contacting one or more outside agencies:

- *Better Business Bureau.* Found in most urban areas throughout Canada, the B.B.B. has considerable information about consumer protection and will investigate complaints and provide information on the business practices of companies.
- *Chamber of Commerce.* Found in most Canadian cities and towns, the Chamber of Commerce is very interested in local business and available to help you with consumer problems.
- *Provincial Consumer Protection Agencies.* All of the provinces and territories have consumer protection agencies. To contact the agency in your province, look in the phone book under the provincial government listing.

Taking Legal Action

As a final step, you may decide that you should contact a lawyer. Depending on the situation, this action may be sufficient to get the other party to settle. If a settlement cannot be reached, you may decide to take the matter to court. When a claim is for a relatively small amount of money, consider taking your action to Small Claims Court.

Choosing a Lawyer

The decision to hire a lawyer is an important one and the selection should be done wisely and with care. Many potential problems can be avoided by obtaining legal advice before you act.

In choosing a lawyer, a good starting place is a strong recommendation from a friend or business association who has encountered a legal problem similar to the one which you are now facing.

Advertising by lawyers is closely regulated, but the law societies in most provinces operate a lawyer referral service which can be contacted by telephone. After explaining your particular problem, you will be referred to a lawyer with an interest in the area of law applicable to your case. Typically the lawyer meets with you for half an hour (the cost of this preliminary interview is generally between $10 and $30, depending on your province of residence). After the initial interview, you are not obligated to hire the lawyer. However, if you choose to do so, the schedule of fees is based on whatever you and the lawyer agree to. Consequently, it is a good idea to discuss fees during the initial interview.

Is a Specialist Needed?

A lawyer in general practice is usually competent to deal with basic legal matters. However, if your problem is complex, the specialist is likely (all things being equal) to achieve a better result than someone who devotes only a part of his or her time to a specialized area of law.

It should be noted that the lawyer-client relationship is absolutely confidential — your lawyer may not divulge any information which you have given him or her without your consent. As well, your lawyer's principal duty is to you, he or she may not enter into any contracts or represent any other client if such actions might be in conflict with your interests.

How Much Will a Lawyer Cost?

Do not be afraid to discuss legal fees with your lawyer during the first meeting. Although it is generally not possible to predict the precise cost of legal services in advance except for straightforward cases, the lawyer can explain how his or her fees are calculated and frequently is able to provide some estimate of costs.

Generally, a lawyer's fee is based primarily on the amount of time spent working on your problem. Depending on such factors as the ability, experience, reputation and area of practice of a particular lawyer, hourly rates may vary from below $40 per hour to above $200 per hour.

In provinces where it is legal, lawyers may agree to accept your case (unless it is a criminal case) on a "contingency fee" basis (that is, the lawyer's fee is based on an agreed-upon percentage of monies won). If the case is lost, nothing or only a small amount is payable. It is important to carefully consider the risks involved and the potential costs and benefits before agreeing to a contingency fee arrangement.

In addition, it should be noted that funding through Legal Aid may be possible, depending on your type of case and whether you qualify for legal assistance (most provinces apply a means or income test while Ontario uses a needs test).

In summary, be careful to read every contract before you sign it. If you are not pleased with a product or service, take action to remedy the situation. Although it is not always possible, try and adopt the philosophy of "buyers-beware" and "buyer-be-aware".

CHAPTER 10

YOUR OWN HOME-BASED BUSINESS

By Lynn Anderson

INTRODUCTION

Can you make money in small business? The answer is a definite yes. The unwritten rule in business is that it takes a well-run business five years to become established and profitable. By starting a business in your home, you can cut this time down dramatically. I have personally met more than one individual who has been making comfortable profits at the end of a year in business. The secret is careful planning and choosing a business that you have the skill to operate.

Today more and more men and women are testing the waters of self-employment. This chapter is geared to individuals who would like to take their hobby and turn it into a business and entrepreneurs who would like to start a home-based business full-time or part-time.

WHO ME?

There is a general mystique concerning entrepreneurs — individuals who own and operate their own business. Basically, the entrepreneur is someone who has assessed his life, his objectives and his personality and decided that "business" is the avenue for him.

Entrepreneurs are characterized by the media as risk-takers, but in reality they have carefully analyzed all the advantages and disadvantages of starting a business.

Some of the advantages are: job satisfaction, recognition for your work, potential financial gain, control over your own life, more challenge, etc. ... The other side of the coin — the disadvantages — are not quite as obvious: you are not eligible for unemployment insurance, business is not a 9-5 job, you must assume responsibility for income taxes, deal with isolation and the possibilities that your business might fail.

Before you consider starting a home-based business, either full-time or part-time, understand what you expect from your business and anticipate some of the problems that could crop up. Talk to other businesspeople, read articles and discuss your ideas with your family.

You can minimize the risks of self-employment in order to maximize the rewards through the development of good business management and a well thought-out business plan.

WHAT KIND OF BUSINESS TO START?

Do you already have a skill or product that someone would pay for? Is there something you would like to learn to do? Take a critical look at yourself — your strengths and your weaknesses. Survey your family and friends for potential ideas for a new business. If you're not sure what you would like to do, there is an excellent book, "168 More Businesses Anyone Can Start And Make A Lot Of Money" (see resource list), that may give you some ideas.

According to Dun & Bradstreet, the largest single cause of business failure in Canada is poor management. If you have no experience in the type of business you propose to start, try working for someone else who is already established. Invest in courses and seminars that will introduce you to skills necessary to run a business.

Will your business be part-time or full-time? Decide how many hours per week you can give to your new venture. Generally, a full-time business requires 60 hours per week (40 hours of work and 20 hours of administration). Most business experts suggest you keep your regular job and start your own business on a part-time basis, so that you'll still have some income during the time you're getting established.

THE BUSINESS PLAN

A common belief is that hard work and a marketable product or service will ensure business success. But without detailed objectives and goals plus a definite time limit, your business could become less then you had hoped for.

A business plan is a guide and a tool to help your business be successful. It is a report on your company, its management, its products and its marketing plans. The business plan describes the present and the future.

Listed below are the steps in developing your business plan. Answer the questions that relate to you.

Type Of Business

A brief description, ie., word processing.

Business Name

Take a look in the yellow pages of your telephone book. There you will find a hodge-podge of businesses trying to make their mark with a business name and hopefully a suitable image.

In picking a name for your business, keep these points in mind:

- Keep it short! A good rule of thumb is two syllables or a phrase that can be said quickly. company names that are short are easier to remember.
- Is it easy to say? A business associate of mine started a company with a name that was difficult to say. It took me a couple of weeks to learn to say it correctly, and I wasn't even a customer. Remember that people are embarrassed if they say names incorrectly and will avoid situations where they might find themselves embarrassed if they say names incorrectly and will avoid situations where they might find themselves embarrassed.
- Keep the spelling simple! All mail and cheques to your company should have the correct spelling of the company name.
- What letter does your company name begin with? If the business name begins with an "A", you will be listed in the telephone book first. The telephone company will alphabetically list businesses in order of letters, then words. For instance, the letters A.S.A.P. come before the word Aamco.

Most customers looking for a service or product will go to the yellow pages and start at the top of the list to find a company to contact. Take a look at your competitors in the yellow pages and decide where you would like to be in the list.

- What kind of image does your company project? Fast? Creative? Quality? Different? Fun?

The image that is associated with your business name also makes a dramatic impact on clients. Use a logo, type of stationery, style of print, and colour to create that image.

For example, take an interior decorating business.

	Approach No. 1	Approach No. 2
Name:	Metamorphose	Transformation
Logo:	Butterfly	Hammer
Colours:	Pink	Grey
Print Style:	Script	Block
Stationery:	Certificate Royal	Bond

Approach Number 1 implies that you will take an ugly caterpillar and transform it into a beautiful butterfly.

Approach Number 2 implies that you will tear down your client's house and make it look different — not necessarily better.

Pick a name for your company that you like, and try it out on friends and relatives. Decide on the image you would like to create. Look at competitors for ideas.

I practiced saying my company name in the shower for days before I decided to pick A.S.A.P. The image I wanted to project was fast, professional and economical word processing. I picked the colours black and white because they were simple and the cheapest to reproduce. My stationery is plain Bond paper — the most economical to buy. The logo is a stop sign with a city sky line inside it. The sun rising implies that I would stay up all night to meet the client's deadline.

Keep these ideas in mind when picking your business name.

Type Of Ownership

Sole Proprietorship: Most home-based businesses are sole proprietorships. There is only one owner. If you choose to operate your business under your own name, it is not necessary to register the business with the province. If you operate your business under a name that is not your own then you must register your business with the province. Contact the Consumer and Commercial Relations department in your area (see resource list).

The advantages of this type of ownership are low start-up costs and the greatest freedom from regulations. The down side is that it is more difficult to raise money and there is the factor of unlimited liability (ie., the business creditors can go after your personal assets to pay bills).

Partnership: A partnership is like a marriage and takes a lot of effort from all parties to make it work. There are two forms of partnerships: limited and general. Limited partners are not liable for partnership debts, beyond their capital contributions. General partners take part in the management of the enterprise and thus are jointly and separately responsible for debts incurred by the partnership.

I am not an advocate of partnerships unless the potential partners have talked to both a lawyer and an accountant to protect the rights of all involved.

Corporation (Limited Company): This type of business structure creates a legal entity. The business has limited liability, ownership is transferable, and it is easier to raise money. But incorporation costs money and incorporated companies are closely regulated.

Incorporation can be done provincially or federally. Check with your provincial Consumer and Commercial Relation department or the Corporations Branch, Consumer and Corporate Affairs Canada, 4th floor, Phase II, Hull, Quebec J8X 4C2.

I would advise most people starting home-based businesses not to consider this type of ownership because of the expense. Talk to an accountant if you have any doubts.

Business Location

Renter or Condominium Owner: If you rent, you must find out if your landlord has restrictions on the use of the property. This also applies to individuals who own a condominium. Some condominium corporations forbid the running of a business on the premises.

If you run into a problem here, you can appeal to the individual(s) in question to grant you an exemption or you can move.

What about the bylaws? Obtain a copy of the bylaws governing home occupations that affect the area you live in. Copies of bylaws are available at your city hall or municipal office. Be sure you understand what these bylaws state. You may have to apply for a "Waiver of Variance" to operate your home-based business legally.

Most bylaws are not that restrictive. Some common criteria for home occupations are:
No noise, health or fire hazard.
No signs.
No employees.
No stock-in trade unless you made it yourself.
No more than one business in the house.
No more than one client can be served at one time.
No more than 25% of the house can be used for the business.

Check with the bylaw people every year to ensure there have been no changes that affect you.

Business License: Check with the municipality to see if you require a business license. Most times you do not.

Products/Services Offered

List all the products/services your business will offer. Avoid the trap of trying to offer too many items. Start off by picking a couple of items — you can always expand your list later.

Price

- What is the going rate (fair market value) for this type of product/service?
- How are you going to be competitive — lower prices or more service for the same dollars? Consumers expect to pay less than fair market value in a home-based business and will exert a great deal of pressure on you to lower your rates.
- Do you have to collect Provincial Sales Tax (PST)? Contact the Retail Sales Tax department to see if you must collect PST. You will need to tell them what products/services the business will offer. If you must collect PST, apply for a vendor's permit.
- Do you have to collect Federal Sales Tax (FST)? The answer is usually no. The rule of thumb is that you must be selling $50,000 per year of taxable items before collecting FST.

Who Is Going To Buy Your Product/Service?

Describe the type of customer who will be interested in what your business has to offer: age, sex, location, associations they might belong to, trade magazines they might read, etc. Design a brochure targeted to this type of customer.

Competitors

Find out who your competitors are. Look in the yellow pages and the newspapers. Where are they located? Phone your competitors and ask them to mail you their brochures. What are the advantages/disadvantages of your competitors? How are you going to stand out?

Cash or Credit

To avoid cash-flow problems, it is always preferable to have cash sales, but if your customers are businesses, then you will have to offer credit, giving them anywhere from 14 to 30 days to pay the invoice in full.

If you wish to explore accepting credit cards, then contact the Bank of Montreal for MasterCard and any bank that accepts Visa. There is usually a yearly rental charge for the loan of the credit card machine, and the bank will supply the necessary slips. The bank also deducts as much as 4% of the total charged per month as a service charge.

Open a Bank Account

Talk to your bank manager about the type of account you should open for your business. Order business cheques.

Business Cards & Stationery

Decide on the image you wish to project through your business stationery. It is not unusual for your business image to evolve in the first year of operation. Keep your costs low for business stationery until you are pleased with the image you are projecting. I suggest:

100 Business Cards
250 Letterheads
250 Envelopes*
1 Stamper
* If cost is a concern, you can purchase a box of legal size white envelopes and stamp your return address in the corner.

Business Telephone

Will you need to have a separate business telephone? It really depends on your business and your clients. But the advantages are:

- You can identify a potential client immediately when the business phone rings. Always answer your business line with enthusiasm. This is something I do not always do with my personal line, when I know the telephone is seldom for me.
- You can attach an answering machine to your business line to handle those times you are unavailable.
- You can use your personal line for out-going calls, freeing up the business line for incoming calls.
- Many clients feel uncomfortable when dealing with a company that does not have "traditional business-like telephone responses". (I lost the battle here many times when my clients heard "Sesame Street" in the background.)

If you choose not to install a separate business line, then contact the telephone company to see if there are any restrictions on using the home line for businesses purposes. Some telephone companies require you to pay the business line rate on your personal telephone line if this phone is being used for business purposes.

Setting Up The Office

If possible, set up your office in an area of your house that will only be used for business. It will make it easier to decide what expenses are business and what expenses are personal. A spare room is ideal. Will you have clients visiting your office? How much surface and storage area will you require?

Some points to keep in mind as you set up your office:

- Your office should be a pleasant environment to work in.
  - Paint the walls with soothing colours like pale pinks, yellows or beiges, avoiding dark moody colours.
  - Have adequate lighting. You will be spending a lot of hours working here, so do not scrimp on lighting.
  - Incorporate plants, posters or paintings into your office
- .Have a large work surface. It is not necessary to buy a desk. I purchased three table tops from a local furniture store and

built a large work surface that also doubled as my desk. If you decide to be creative in building your work surface area, you could save money and end up with a design that will suit the room you are in.

- Make sure that your desk/work surface is organized and that everything is within reach.
- Install a phone.
- Invest in a good comfortable chair.
- Have all of your supplies organized in a manner that makes it easy to see what is there.
- Allow for plenty of storage space. Depending on your type of business you may need bookshelves or a method of neatly storing your material.
- Every business requires a file cabinet at some point. It is an excellent way to store information about your clients, your bills and your correspondence. Used filing cabinets are readily available through surplus stores or in the newspaper.
- Visit the local stationery store and pick up a catalogue. There are many supplies available today that could assist you in business from cardboard filing boxes to shopping bags.

On average, you will be spending 48-60 hours a week in your office if you are running the business full-time. Take the time to plan your office before you start.

By dedicating an area of your residence to business, you can now claim some of your household expenses as business expenses. The general rule of thumb is to:

find the total sq. ft. of your home:	800 sq. ft.
find the total sq. ft. of your office:	200 sq. ft.
find the percentage:	$(200/800) \times 100 = 25.0\%$

For business purposes, you can now claim this percentage (25%) of your household expenses, such as:

- all utilities
- rent or mortgage interest (the principal is not deductible)
- property taxes
- maintenance costs (repainting, etc.)

Marketing For Home-Based Business

Yellow Pages. How do you as a consumer shop? You probably use the yellow pages of your telephone book. If you are looking for a florist, you'll turn to that section, scan the ads until one catches your eye and then telephone them.

Many home-based businesses underestimate the value of a

listing or an ad in the yellow pages. When I started my word processing firm three years ago, I decided, quite by accident, that the only way I could compete with 50 other firms was to advertise like them. So with my hand clutched around my virgin cheque book, I created a large ad that cost me $1,100 for the first year. My intuition was right. My advertisement paid for itself in three months. In 1987, it paid for itself in two months.

It can work for you too! Find out who your competitors are. Look at their advertising. Design your own ad or seek the assistance of the telephone company. Be objective when looking at your own ad. Show it to friends, relatives, clients. Make sure you are completely satisfied. Keep in mind that telephone books are printed once a year so you won't be able to change your mind for at least 12 months.

Personal Marketing: Get out of your office/home and join organizations and associations. Through experience you will learn that word-of-mouth is the strongest marketing a business can employ. This method of selling is even more important for the home-based business. You must control the amount of business you receive so that you can perform the service or deliver the product. Let's face it, most home-based businesses are working with one or two principals that also do the accounting, marketing, banking, designing and serve as the janitor(s).

I spend $500 a year on memberships in business associations and attend nearly ever activity I can. My goal each time is to meet at least two new associates and let them know about me. The sales generated by this form of marketing pays for the membership fees and much more each year.

I have only used these two marketing methods to build my company. My sales have grown at a steady and controlled rate and I now employ three full-time people. These methods can work for you too. Give them a try.

How Much Money Is Enough?

One of the hardest factors to speculate on is operating capital. How much money do I need to run my business every month?

If the business relies on you to perform the service or make the product, anything that prevents you from doing this work is going to hurt monthly sales. The delay between buying the supplies, making the product and being paid for that service can cause major cash flow problems as well.

It is important to anticipate months that you will be short of funds to cover your expenses and have back-up resources to fall back on — perhaps a line of credit at the bank or personal savings. This is done by using cash flow statements which in reality are a break-down of the total expected money during any period (revenue) minus the total expected bills during the same period (expenses). The difference should be positive (meaning you have the money!). Learn how to use cash flow statements now. You will be using this tool a great deal in business. Visit a book store and invest in an accounting book that discusses cash flow statements in detail. Banks also have brochures and samples of cash flow statements.

Estimate your costs for the first six months:

Equipment and Furniture
- List what your basic requirements are.
- What is the cost involved.

Start-up Costs
- These are usually one-time charges, like installing a business phone, increasing insurance needs, having a brochure printed, purchasing opening inventory/supplies, etc.

Operating Needs for 6 Months
- Estimate or guess how much money you will need to run your business for the first six months, assuming the business has no sales during this time.
- This technique allows room for errors in estimating and helps reduce some of the stress of meeting any expenses.

Total (a) + (b) + (c) = Enough Money!

If you can finance your business through personal funds, you'll find this is the easiest way. Borrowing money from a bank is the next option.

Visit your bank manager and discuss a possible loan for your business. Your bank manager may suggest a personal loan if the amount is small. He will also explain what type of paperwork the bank will require from you. Generally you will have to prepare a business plan which contains the following information:

- the amount of the loan
- how you are going to spend the money

- how you are going to repay the loan
- a personal financial statement
- a description of your business concept (why are you starting the business)
- a description of your market (who are your clients going to be)
- a description of your marketing plans (how are you going to sell to your clients)
- financial statements for your business (balance sheet, income statement)
- projected cash flow statements for your business

You should seek the services of an accountant to help you prepare financial statements for your business.

Keep in mind when you are financing your business through a bank that it is generally easy to finance a new business if you have a good business plan. To borrow money later from a bank, you must be showing a profit and a healthy growth.

Credit Ratings

Open up accounts with suppliers and establish a credit rating for your business. You might like to visit your local Credit Bureau to see your files. Ensure the information is correct. Consider opening a file for your business. Remember that businesses wanting to check on your credit rating will use the services of the Credit Bureau.

Income Tax

Revenue Canada has numerous bulletins and brochures for the self-employed person. Request a copy of these publications.

A business must keep records of sales and expenses ɹr Revenue Canada. These records must support the figure: ᴉn your income tax form for declared profit or loss.

There are plenty of reference books in the library on accounting. It doesn't hurt to talk to an accountant and have him/her help you set up a bookkeeping system.

Finding Experts

Talk to other business people to learn what they are doing and the mistakes they have made. I regularly invite business associates I want to meet to lunch and am constantly learning new methods of doing business. I use these lunches to bounce ideas off others and get some objective feedback.

Find a bank manager, a lawyer and an accountant that you like. You may not immediately need their services, but they can become invaluable sources of information.

Resources

Library

Too often businesspeople ignore the local library as a valuable source of information. The library has listings of Canadian businesses by location and business type. There are countless books covering all subjects relating to business, and copies of trade magazines and newspapers. Have the Reference Librarian explain how to use the services of the reference library. It can be "one-stop shopping" for information.

Books

Here is a short list of books you will find interesting:
(1)   "Minding Your Own Business", from any branch of the Federal Business Development Bank
(2)   "You Can Make Big Money At Home", Ronald J. Cooke, Fitzhenry & Whiteside
(3)   "Small Business Survival Guide", Joseph Mancusso, Prentice-Hall
(4)   "168 More Businesses Anyone Can Start And Make A Lot of Money", Chase Revel, Bantam Books

Business Regulations/Services

Dept. of Consumer & Corporate Affairs Canada, Place du Portage, Tower 2, Ottawa-Hull, ON K1A 0C9

Dept. of Regional Industrial Expansion, Business Centre, 235 Queen Street, Ottawa, ON K1A 0H5

Federal Business Development Bank, 901 Victoria Sq., Montreal, PQ H2Z 1R1

Revenue Canada, Taxation, Information Services Branch, 875 Heron Road, Ottawa, ON K1A 0L8

Statistics Canada, Ottawa, ON K1A 0T6

Alta.: Dept. of Consumer & Corporate Affairs, Information Services, Box 1616, Edmonton, AB T5J 2N9

Dept. of Tourism & Small Business, Small Business Division, 15th Fl., Capitol Square, 10065 Jasper Avenue, Edmonton, AB T5J 0H4

B.C.: Registrar of Companies, Ministry of Consumer & Corporate Affairs, 940 Blanshard St., Waddington Bldg., Victoria, BC V8W 3E6

Ministry of Industry & Small Business Development, Trade & Industry Division, No. 140, 800 Hornby St., Vancouver, BC V6Z 2C5

Man.: Dept. of Consumer & Corporate Affairs, Office of the Deputy Minister, No. 336, Legislative Bldg., Winnipeg, MB R3C 0V8

Corporations & Business Names Branch, Dept. of Consumer & Corporate Affairs, 10th Fl., Woodsworth Bldg., Winnipeg, MB RC3 3L6

Industry Branch, Manitoba Industry, Trade & Technology, 7th Fl., 155 Carlton St., Winnipeg, MB R3C 3H8

N.B.: Consumer Affairs Branch, Dept. of Justice, Box 6000, Fredericton, NB E3B 5H1

Nfld.: Director of Commercial Relations, Dept. of Consumer Affairs & Communications, Confederation Bldg., Box 4750, St. John's, NF A1C 517

Ont.: Companies Branch, Ministry of Consumer & Commercial Relations, 555 Yonge St., Toronto, ON M7A 2H6

Metro Toronto: Metropolitan Licensing Commission, 20 Holly St., Toronto, ON M4S 3B1

P.E.I.: Corporations Division, Dept. of Justice, Box 2000, Charlottetown, PEI C1A 7N8

Que.: Communications, Ministère de l'Industrie et du Commerce, 710 Place d'Youville, Québec, PQ G1R 4Y4

Montreal: CIDEM — Business Development, 155 Notre Dame est, Montréal, PQ H2Y 1B5

Sask.: Saskatchewan Consumer & Commercial Affairs, 1871 Smith St., Regina, SK S4P 3V7

Communications & Development, Dept. of Co-operation & Co-operative Development, 2055 Albert St., Regina, SK S4P 3V7

Yukon: Consumer & Corporate Affairs, Box 2703, Whitehorse, YT Y1A 2C6

Magazines

"Alberta Business", Canasus Communications Inc., 209-603 7th Ave. S.W., Calgary, AB T2P 2T5

"Atlantic Business", Canasus Communications Inc., 3030-7001 Mumford Rd., Halifax, NS B3L 4R3

"The Bottom Line", Bottom Line Publications Inc., 341 Steelcase Rd. W., Markham, ON L3R 3W1

"B.C. Business", Canasus Communications, 550 Burrard St., 2nd Fl., Vancouver, BC V6C 2J6

"Business & Finance in Ontario", Business & Finance in Ontario Publishers Inc., 205 Riviera Dr., Unit 1, Markham, ON L3R 2L6

"Canadian Business", CB Media Ltd., 70 The Esplanade, 2nd Fl., Toronto, ON M5E 1R2

"Durham Classified Business Directory & Consumers Guide", Lloyd's Local Directories, P.O. Box 262, West Hill, ON M1E 4R5

"Enterprise", P.O. Box 2038, 1441 Creekside Dr., Vancouver, BC V6B 3R9

"Small Business", Financial Post (Div. Maclean Hunter Ltd.) Maclean Hunter Bldg., 777 Bay St., Toronto, ON M5W 1A7

Associations

Assn. of Canadian Venture Capital Companies, c/o Archie MacKinnon, Alta-Can Tele-Com Inc., 411-1st St. S.E., Calgary, AB T2G 4Y5

Canadian Assn. of Women Business Owners, 69 Sherbourne St., Suite 222, Toronto, ON M5A 3X7

Canadian Federation of Independent Business, 4141 Yonge Street, Suite 101, Willowdale, ON M2P 2A6

Canadian Organization of Small Business, 1100 Royal Trust Tower, Edmonton Centre, Edmonton, AB T5J 2Z1; 7050 Woodbine Avenue, Suite 310, Markham, ON L3R 4G8

The Small Business Network Inc., 52 Sheppard Ave. W., Suite 100, Willowdale, ON M2N 1M2

A-LINE, a non-profit association for home-based businesses, 20 Hobart Crescent, Nepean, ON K2H 5S4

The Home Businesswomen's Network, 195 Markville Rd., Unionville, ON L3R 4V8

Miscellaneous: contact the Better Business Bureau and the Chamber of Commerce in your area as well.

Appendix

Financing The Canada Pension Plan

The Schedule of Contribution Rates to CPP

Year	Rate* (%)	Year	Rate* (%)	Year	Rate* (%)	Year	Rate* (%)	Year	Rate* (%)
1987	3.80	1992	4.75	1997	5.50	2002	6.25	2007	7.00
1988	4.00	1993	4.90	1998	5.65	2003	6.40	2008	7.15
1989	4.20	1994	5.05	1999	5.80	2004	6.55	2009	7.30
1990	4.40	1995	5.20	2000	5.95	2005	6.70	2010	7.45
1991	4.60	1996	5.35	2001	6.10	2006	6.85	2011	7.60

Example of increases in CPP contributions for workers earning average wages* during the first 10 years of the new schedule.

	New Contribution Rate (%)	Total Maximum Yearly Contributions* Under Old Arrangements	After New Arrangements	Amount of Annual Increase in Contributions
			(dollars)	
1987	3.8	421.20	444.60	23.40
1988	4.0	437.40	486.00	48.60
1989	4.2	453.60	529.20	75.60
1990	4.4	471.60	576.40	104.80
1991	4.6	489.60	625.60	136.00

* Assumes a 4% annual increase in average wages after 1987.
Source: Health and Welfare Canada

Net Worth Statement

List the current market value of your:

ASSETS	Yours	Joint	Spouse
Liquid Assets			
• Cash and bank accounts			
• Canada Savings Bonds			
• Life Insurance cash value			
• Short Term deposits			
Semiliquid Assets			
• Stocks and Bonds			
• Medium Term Deposits			
• Money owed to you			
Retirement Assets			
• RPP (Employer Pension Plan)			
• RRSP (Registered Retirement Savings)			
• DPSP (Deferred Profit Sharing)			
Business Interests			
Personal Property			
• Art, Antiques, Jewelry			
• Automobiles			
• Other			
Real Estate			
• House			
• Vacation Home or other			
TOTAL ASSETS (A)			

TOTAL ASSETS (A)

LIABILITIES	Yours	Joint	Spouse
• Bank debt			
• Mortgages			
• Credit Card Debt			
• Margin Accounts			
• Income Tax Owing			
• Life Insurance Loans			
• Other			
Total Liabilities (B)			
Subtract (B) from (A):			
= NET WORTH			

Summary:
Family Assets _____
Family Liabilities _____
Family Net Worth _____

(This chart is provided courtesy of the Women's Financial Planning Centre, 2602-2 Bloor Street West, Toronto, Ontario M4W 3E2.)

Goal Setting

Personal and Family Objectives

Financial

Short Term (up to 1 year) -..................................
....
Medium Term (1-5 years) -..............................
....
Long Term (5-10 years) -..............................
....

Career

Short Term -...
....
Medium Term -.......................................
....
Long Term -...
....

Educational

Short Term -...
....
Medium Term -.......................................
....
Long Term -...
....

Personal

Short Term -...
....
Medium Term -.......................................
....
Long Term -...
....

Goal setting should be completed as an individual activity and a family activity.

Projected Family Budget

Expenses

Savings: $ _____ $ _____

Home:
Rent-Mortgage Payment $ _____
Taxes on Property $ _____
Insurance on Home $ _____
Repairs & Decorating $ _____
Heat $ _____
Utilities $ _____
Telephone $ _____
Appliance Replacement $ _____ $ _____

Food:
Groceries $ _____
Meat $ _____
Milk $ _____
Outside Meals $ _____ $ _____

Medical:
Prov. Hospital Premiums $ _____
Supplementary Health Plan $ _____
Drugs $ _____
Dentist & Orthodontist $ _____
Optician & Glasses $ _____ $ _____

Clothing:
Clothes $ _____
Footwear $ _____
Dry Cleaning $ _____ $ _____

Transportation:
Car Payment-Own/Rent $ _____
Car Insurance & Licence $ _____
Maintenance $ _____ $ _____

Miscellaneous:

Entertainment	$ _____	
Vacation	$ _____	
Special Occasions		
Christmas, Birthdays, etc.	$ _____	
Contributions	$ _____	
Education	$ _____	
Revolving Charge Account	$ _____	
Other	$ _____	$ _____

Total Monthly Budget $ _____

Net Income: wage(s), pension(s), investment and/or rental income, etc. $ _____

Net Surplus: $ _____

INFLATION/INTEREST TABLE

Year	Inflation/Interest Factors at Year End				
	4%	6%	8%	10%	12%
1	1.04	1.06	1.08	1.10	1.12
2	1.08	1.12	1.17	1.21	1.25
3	1.12	1.19	1.26	1.33	1.40
4	1.17	1.26	1.36	1.46	1.57
5	1.22	1.34	1.47	1.61	1.76
6	1.27	1.42	1.59	1.77	1.97
7	1.32	1.50	1.71	1.95	2.21
8	1.37	1.59	1.85	2.14	2.48
9	1.42	1.69	2.00	2.36	2.77
10	1.48	1.79	2.16	2.59	3.11
11	1.54	1.90	2.33	2.85	3.48
12	1.60	2.01	2.52	3.14	3.90
13	1.67	2.13	2.72	3.45	4.36
14	1.73	2.26	2.94	3.80	4.89
15	1.80	2.40	3.17	4.18	5.47
16	1.87	2.54	3.43	4.59	6.13
17	1.95	2.69	3.70	5.05	6.87
18	2.03	2.85	4.00	5.56	7.69
19	2.11	3.03	4.32	6.12	8.61
20	2.19	3.21	4.66	6.73	9.65
21	2.28	3.40	5.03	7.40	10.80
22	2.37	3.60	5.44	8.14	12.10
23	2.46	3.82	5.87	8.95	13.55
24	2.56	4.05	6.34	9.85	15.18
25	2.67	4.29	6.85	10.83	17.00
26	2.77	4.55	7.40	11.92	19.04
27	2.88	4.82	7.99	13.11	21.32
28	3.00	5.11	8.63	14.42	23.88
29	3.12	5.42	9.32	15.86	26.75
30	3.24	5.74	10.06	17.45	29.96
31	3.37	6.09	10.87	19.19	33.56
32	3.51	6.45	11.74	21.11	37.58
33	3.65	6.84	12.68	23.23	42.09
34	3.79	7.25	13.69	25.55	47.14
35	3.95	7.69	14.79	28.10	52.80
36	4.10	8.15	15.97	30.91	59.14
37	4.27	8.64	17.25	34.00	66.23
38	4.44	9.15	18.63	37.40	74.18
39	4.62	9.70	20.12	41.14	83.08
40	4.80	10.29	21.72	45.26	93.05
41	4.99	10.90	23.46	49.79	104.22
42	5.19	11.56	25.34	54.76	116.72
43	5.40	12.25	27.37	60.24	130.73
44	5.62	12.99	29.56	66.26	146.42
45	5.84	13.76	31.92	72.89	163.99
46	6.07	14.59	34.47	80.18	183.67
47	6.32	15.47	37.23	88.20	205.71
48	6.57	16.39	40.21	97.02	230.39
49	6.83	17.38	43.43	106.72	258.04
50	7.11	18.42	46.90	117.39	289.00
51	7.39	19.53	50.65	129.13	323.68
52	7.69	20.70	54.71	142.04	362.52
53	7.99	21.94	59.08	156.25	406.03
54	8.31	23.26	63.81	171.87	454.75
55	8.65	24.65	68.91	189.06	509.32
56	8.99	26.13	74.43	207.97	570.44
57	9.35	27.70	80.38	228.76	638.89
58	9.73	29.36	86.81	251.64	715.56
59	10.12	31.12	93.76	276.80	801.43
60	10.52	32.99	101.26	304.48	897.60

1987 Rates of Provincial and Territorial Income Tax

These rates are to be applied to Basic Federal Tax.
The rates may be subject to change during 1987.

Newfoundland	60%
Prince Edward Island	55%
Nova Scotia	56.5%
New Brunswick	58%
Quebec	not applicable
Ontario	50%
Manitoba	54%
Saskatchewan	50%
Alberta	46.5%
British Columbia	51.5%
Northwest Territories	43%
Yukon Territory	45%

Exemptions and Deductions Switched to Credits

A system of tax credits will replace most of the 1987 personal deductions for 1988.

	1987 Deduction	1988 Tax Credit
Basic Personal	$4,220	$1,020
Married, Equivalent	3,700	850
Child/Dependants Under 18	560	65
Child 18 & Over	1,200	0
Age 65, Disability	2,640, 2,920	550
Pension Income	1,000	17% (max. $170)
Employment Deduction	500	0
Education Deduction	50/month	10/month
Charitable Donations	20% of net income	17 or 29% of donation

Tax-Assisted Retirement Savings

Effective January 1, 1989 the contribution limit of 18% of earnings will start. For 1988, the dollar limits are the same as the 1987 limits. Changes from 1989 forward are noted on the following chart:

Dollar Limits on Tax-Assisted Retirement Savings

Year	Previous Proposal		New Proposal		
	RPP	RRSP	DPSP	RPP	RRSP
1987	$ 7,000	$ 7,500	$3,500	$ 7,000	$ 7,500
1988	11,500	9,500	3,500	7,000	7,500
1989	13,500	11,500	5,250	10,500	8,500
1990	15,500	13,500	5,750	11,500	10,500
1991		15,500	6,250	12,500	11,500
1992			6,750	13,500	12,500
1993			7,250	14,500	13,500
1994			7,750	15,500	14,500
1995			indexed	indexed	15,500

Note: The RPP amounts are for money-purchase plans. There is no limit on required contributions to defined benefit RPPs since there are limits on the size of the tax-assisted pension benefits such a plan can provide.

Rave Reviews

Here's what readers have said about *Guide To Making Money,* the first edition. Let us know what you think about this all-new second volume.

"I look forward to overhauling my financial situation based on some of the comprehensive advice contained in the *Guide To Making Money.*"
Michael Sale, Scarborough, Ontario

"I think every home should have this book."
Don Bell, Willowdale, Ontario

"Unusual approach — access to authors — great!"
Marilyn Wheeler, Gananoque, Ontario

"By far the best book on money management that I have ever read."
Morris Shane, C.A., Montreal, Quebec

"It has given me many ideas and new insight on how to invest money."
Ann Hines, Toronto, Ontario

"Should be in every conscientious individual's possession."
W.M. Pittingill, Brighton, Ontario

"This is a very good book especially for the person with little knowledge of financial planning."
Peggy Eddolls, High River, Alberta

"It answered many questions that I always wanted to ask but never had time to do so."
Ostap Halin, Calgary, Alberta

"Very easy to find any and every subject because of the detailed contents and logical progression of topics."
Lidia Edwards, Pitt Meadows, British Columbia

"Income tax information presented in an easy-to-understand manner. The Government should hire some of you to rewrite the Act!"

Roy Cowan, Chilliwack, British Columbia

"Best book I've ever read. It explains well, simply and concisely with enough information and not too detailed. As a pension fund administrator..."

J.M. Fortier, Montreal, Quebec

"There are many helpful suggestions on ways to save money such as..."

Charles Lyons, Doaktown, New Brunswick

"The authors bring the complicated world of finance closer to the average person."

James Breti, Punnichy, Saskatchewan

"One of the best (financial) books that I have ever read, and one that I would recommend every person should read."

Gladys Reid, Lower Sackville, Nova Scotia

"This is a very practical and informative book ... excellent information that applies to Canada."

Betty Laing, Winnipeg, Manitoba

"I found the *Guide To Making Money* extremely informative and written in a fashion that is completely comprehensible to the lay person. It will assist me greatly with respect to my retirement plans."

Dennis Huyda, Winnipeg, Manitoba

Invest In Yourself

Reading the *Canadian MoneySaver* pays off. You profit from our advice or we'll return your money! That's right. You have a money-back guarantee for the life of your subscription.

The authors of *Guide To Making Money* are contributors to the *Canadian MoneySaver* magazine. Our remarkable team of contributing editors includes five dozen of Canada's most astute financial experts. They provide you with the inside information and practical advice you can act on immediately to reach your personal goals.

This practical guide about money matters is a personal finance magazine which carries no advertising. Since September, 1981 we have been supported by our readers' subscription fees. We work for thousands of Canadians. We'll work for you, too.

Let Canada's top financial minds work to defend, stretch and multiply your hard-earned dollars. You learn how to make your money grow through:
- smart use of personal finances
- investment ideas that work
- wise tax and retirement planning
- travel savings and discounts
- understanding your pensions/benefits
- profitable small/home business practices
- best consumer bargains, and more...

As a reader of this book, you are eligible for our lowest introductory subscription price — only $12. You receive 9 issues (1 year) for less than half the basic price of $24.75. You save $12.75!

USE THIS COUPON TODAY TO SAVE MONEY

Yes, I wish to keep making money. I understand that you offer a 100% money-back guarantee.

☐ I enclose $12. ☐ Cheque/MO ☐ Visa ☐ MasterCard
Send me 9 issues

☐ Send me a Visa/MC No._____
free copy. Card Expiry Date_____

Name: _____
(Please print)
Address: _____

Mail/Payable to: MoneySaver, Box 370, Bath, Ontario K0H 1G0 (613) 352-7448

You Profit
By Keeping In Touch

Reading the *Canadian MoneySaver* pays off. You profit by keeping informed and up-to-date on an ongoing basis.

Write or call us today for a *free* current copy of the *Canadian MoneySaver*. We will also include our personal finance library — a listing of several financial books written by contributors to the *Canadian MoneySaver*.

Canadian MoneySaver, P.O. Box 370, Bath, Ontario K0H 1G0 (613) 352-7448

If you have the time, we would like to know what you think of *Guide To Making Money*.

Comments: _____

_____

_____

_____

_____

_____

_____

_____

_____

_____

_____

May we quote your comments in our advertising?
(   ) Yes (   ) No

Name: _____
(Please print)
Address: _____

_____

(City)   Province   P. Code